D1557167

Women with a Mission

RELIGION AND AMERICAN CULTURE

Women with a Mission

Religion, Gender, and the Politics of Women Clergy

Laura R. Olson, Sue E. S. Crawford, and Melissa M. Deckman

THE UNIVERSITY OF ALABAMA PRESS

Tuscaloosa

Copyright © 2005
The University of Alabama Press
Tuscaloosa, Alabama 35487-0380
All rights reserved
Manufactured in the United States of America

Typeface: ACaslon

∞
The paper on which this book is printed meets the minimum requirements of American National Standard for Information Science—Permanence of Paper for Printed Library Materials, ANSI Z39.48–1984.

Library of Congress Cataloging-in-Publication Data

Olson, Laura R., 1967–
    Women with a mission : religion, gender, and the politics of women clergy / Laura R. Olson, Sue E. S. Crawford, and Melissa M. Deckman.
        p. cm. — (Religion and American culture)
    Includes bibliographical references and index.
    ISBN 0-8173-1460-1 (cloth : alk. paper)
        1. Women clergy—United States—Political activity. 2. Women rabbis—United States—Political activity. 3. Women in politics—United States. 4. Religion and politics—United States. I. Crawford, Sue E. S., 1967– II. Deckman, Melissa M. (Melissa Marie), 1971– III. Title. IV. Religion and American culture (Tuscaloosa, Ala.)
    BL65.P7O395 2005
    323′.042′0882621—dc22

                                                    2004025702

To women clergy in our lives and everywhere

Contents

List of Tables and Figures   ix

Preface and Acknowledgments   xi

1. Women with a Mission   1

2. The Components of Clergywomen's Political Mobilization   14

3. Religion, Gender, and the Social Justice Mission   33

4. Clergywomen's Political Priorities   57

5. Clergywomen's Political Action Agendas   77

6. Clergywomen's Political Strategies   100

7. Prospects for the Future   137

Notes   149

Bibliography   173

Index   185

Tables and Figures

Table 1.1 Numbers and Percentages of Clergywomen in Eight Religious Traditions over Time   8

Table 2.1 Demographic Comparison of Four-City and National Samples   21

Table 3.1 Clergywomen's Views on Gender and Politics (National Survey Sample)   50

Table 4.1 Clergywomen's Political Priorities (Urban Interview Sample)   59

Table 4.2 Clergywomen's Political Priorities (National Survey Sample)   60

Table 5.1 Clergywomen's Action Agendas (Urban Interview Sample)   79

Table 5.2 Clergywomen's Action Agendas (National Survey Sample)   80

Table 5.3 Priority–Action Agenda Comparison   82

Table 5.4 Priority-Action Consistency and Inconsistency (Urban Interview Sample)   85

Table 6.1 Approval and Use of Cue-Giving Strategies   106

Table 6.2 Approval and Use of Direct-Action Strategies   110

Table 6.3 Strategies by City (Urban Interview Sample)   124

Table 6.4 Cue-Giving Mobilization   126

Table 6.5 Direct-Action Mobilization   127

Figure 2.1 Political Mobilization Framework   26

Preface and Acknowledgments

American politics has felt the shaping hand of clergy since colonial times. Despite the theoretical separation of church and state in the United States, religious leaders have influenced myriad political discourses and led a full range of political movements. One of the most important transformations of the American ministry and rabbinate in the past century has been the influx of women into clergy positions. No longer is it accurate to refer to the political influence of "clergymen." Instead, we must now acknowledge and take stock of the ways in which growing numbers of clergywomen are shaping the American religious and political landscapes. It is the purpose of this book to undertake precisely these tasks.

Our shared interest in the study of clergy and politics has been motivated by the many intellectual puzzles that the connection between religion and politics in the United States can help to illuminate. Generally speaking, studying clergy and their political choices provides a window for understanding the connections between work and politics. All three of us have had a sustained interest in how the context of daily work life influences the political interests and behaviors of elites. Women clergy have been of particular interest to us, as the significance of the recent growth in the number of women in clergy positions cannot be understated. Some seminary classes now enroll more women students than men. The changing gender dynamics within religious traditions that ordain women are bound to have political implications. We also have been struck by the strength and relative homogeneity of clergywomen's political views. The title of this book, *Women with a Mission,* was inspired by the powerful and palpable commitment that so many of these women have to the political fight for social justice.

Academia can be an isolating world in some respects, but it can also foster wonderful collaborations and friendships. Our journey together began in 1997 when Laura Olson and Sue Crawford met on a panel at the annual meeting of the Midwest Political Science Association in Chicago. Both of us were searching for the "next big idea" to research following our doctoral dissertations (both of which examined clergy as political elites), and a cup of coffee after the panel happily turned into a multiyear project. Later in 1997, Laura reconnected with Melissa Deckman at the annual meeting of the Southern Political Science Association in Norfolk. We had first met when Laura interviewed for a faculty position at American University, where Melissa was completing her doctorate. Over lunch, Melissa presented the idea of pursuing a study of women clergy. Soon thereafter, the three of us became a research team, and even more significantly, friends. As the years went by and our project developed, we shared hundreds (perhaps thousands) of e-mails, scores of telephone calls, and several productive and enjoyable "writing summits" at our respective homes in South Carolina, Nebraska, and Maryland.

We owe professional and personal debts to the many people who have assisted us along the way as we pursued this research project. Neither the research nor the book that has resulted from it would have been possible without the generous cooperation of the many women clergy whom we interviewed. We are ever grateful for their willingness to spend time with us sharing their stories and filling out our surveys. Their accounts— and their genuine interest in our project—have inspired, encouraged, and sustained our work on this book. It is our hope that we have represented them accurately.

We would also like to acknowledge our colleagues and students at Clemson University, Creighton University, and Washington College for their support and interest. All three of us work with fine people in departments that allow us to do the sort of work we wish to do. Particular thanks are due to several students who assisted us with data collection and transcription and worked with us on conference papers early in this project: at Creighton University, Christi Braun, Kristin (Kadleck) Zurek, and Natasha Mertz, and at Washington College, Tracey Stewart. Many thanks are also due to Joleen Richwine for her work transcribing interviews and Christy Rowan for her assistance with the survey we did of Disciples of Christ clergy. The careful attention that all of these individuals gave to detail allowed us to spend more time developing the analysis that became the heart of this book.

We are also grateful for the generous research support we received from a variety of sources. Laura Olson was able to spend time working on the project during the 1999–2000 academic year as a visiting research fellow at the Center for the Study of Religion at Princeton University. While at Princeton I received invaluable advice, input, and support from Bob Wuthnow and the participants in the weekly Religion and Culture Workshop, particularly Wendy Cadge. I am also deeply grateful to the Louisville Institute for a 2001 Summer Stipend Grant that allowed me to spend extensive time working on an early draft of this manuscript. Moreover, the Disciples of Christ survey was funded in part by a grant I received from the Society for the Scientific Study of Religion in 2000, as well as by my department at Clemson University. Sue Crawford wishes to thank the Creighton University Graduate School and the Creighton University College of Arts and Sciences for their financial support. Melissa Deckman thanks the Association for the Sociology of Religion for a Fichter Grant that partially funded the Disciples of Christ survey in 2000. I am also grateful to Washington College for awarding me a Faculty Enhancement Grant that provided funds and assistance for this project, as well as the Gender Studies Department at Washington College for sponsoring a public talk about this book.

We have benefited greatly from the wisdom and encouragement of our colleagues in the Religion and Politics section of the American Political Science Association. Our personal and professional relationships with others in our subfield have made this research project substantially sounder and more enjoyable. The care and attention that senior scholars in the section give to mentoring and supporting junior scholars are perhaps unparalleled in the field of political science. In particular, Corwin Smidt, Jim Guth, Ted Jelen, John Green, and Booth Fowler believed in this project from the start and offered support and constructive criticism along the way. Corwin Smidt deserves additional thanks for organizing the Cooperative Clergy survey project that generated the national data we use in the book. On that note, we wish to thank all of the participants in the Cooperative Clergy project who gathered data on mainline Protestant ministers, with special thanks to John Green for his additional help with related projects. We have also gained much from the discussions we have had with our good friend and colleague Paul Djupe about how to push the study of clergy and politics in new directions. And we wish to thank Dan Waterman at the University of Alabama Press; our excellent copy editor, Lady Vowell Smith; as well as the various anonymous reviewers who have offered thorough, fair, and helpful commentary on our manuscripts (especially this one) along the way.

Finally, the unconditional encouragement and support we receive from our families and friends have been essential to the success of this project. We cannot begin to list all of the ways in which they have made this book possible, nor even list all of the many people in our lives who fit in this category. But our parents—Mary and Bob Olson, Mary and Thomas Steinhauser, and Diann and Lloyd Deckman—and family members—especially Matt Olson, David Crawford, Nathan Crawford, Philip Crawford, and Sean Fallon—deserve special thanks for the many things they have done for us. Several special clergywomen have also touched our lives, including Diane Carroll, Julie Murdoch, Stephanie Tucker, and Sarah Wood, and we thank them for their inspiration and guidance. We dedicate this book to clergywomen in our lives and everywhere.

Women with a Mission

1
Women with a Mission

Rabbi Julia Goldstein[1] sits on a community board of directors for a local hospital, a position that often finds her lobbying at the state capitol to raise funds and awareness about organ donations, emergency services, and blood drives. Rev. Annette Martin is a warrior for abortion rights. She dedicates substantial time to demonstrating, lobbying, and testifying before state legislative committees on behalf of a religious pro-choice organization. Rev. Mary Ruth Wilson oversees the delivery of a multitude of social services that are provided to the less fortunate by various ministries of her congregation. Choosing to serve in a working-poor neighborhood near the inner city, Rev. Geraldine Smith sees her presence in this community as an essential element of her ministry as she strives to be a voice for people who live in her church's neighborhood. In addition to her pastoral duties, she serves on various city coalitions and task forces. All of these women are part of an emerging new vanguard within the American ministry: female pastors and rabbis who feel variously called to participate in politics. What are the forces that propel these women into the political world—and in some instances, keep them from it?

The simple fact of being a female religious leader carries political connotations. Today's clergywomen have cause to feel feminist bonds of sisterhood with the early pioneers of the political struggle for women's equality in the United States. Even before the nation was born, Anne Hutchinson was excommunicated from the Massachusetts Bay Colony for claiming that she had received and could interpret God's revelation.[2]

In 1848, Seneca Falls, New York, played host to one of the first organized public discussions of women's rights. One of the many resolutions debated at Seneca Falls during the drafting of the *Declaration of Sentiments and Resolutions* stated "That the speedy success of our course depends upon the zealous and untiring efforts of both men and women, for the overthrow of the monopoly of the pulpit, and for the securing to women an equal participation with men in the various trades, professions, and commerce."[3] A generation after Seneca Falls, Frances Willard, founder of the Woman's Christian Temperance Union, saw fit to publish a book entitled *Woman in the Pulpit*.[4] It is telling that women's acceptance into the male-dominated ministry has been seen from the outset as an important prong of women's equality.

Even though they were barred from the pulpit for generations, women have played integral roles throughout the history of American religion by teaching Sunday school, cooking meals, volunteering for myriad projects, and serving on altar guilds. In the Roman Catholic Church, women religious (nuns) have also served faithfully in important official roles, such as teaching in parochial schools.[5] Historically women have also been more likely than men to attend religious services in the United States.[6] Despite women's many contributions to American religion, however, it took generations of struggle before they were allowed to enter the ordained ministry even in small numbers. And there is still no consensus in American religious circles about whether the Bible allows or prohibits women's ordination. Christian opponents of women's ordination point to scriptural passages including 1 Timothy 2:11–12, which says: "Let a woman learn in silence with all submissiveness. I permit no woman to teach or to have authority over men; she is to keep silent."[7] However, proponents who argue for women's ordination in Christian denominations point to such passages as Galatians 3:28: "There is neither Jew nor Greek, there is neither slave nor free, there is neither male nor female; for you are all one in Christ Jesus."[8] Despite the disagreement, the pulpit recently has become more hospitable to women within both Christianity and Judaism.[9] Women now constitute about 10 percent of all American religious leaders—and their ranks continue to expand[10]—but controversy remains in many traditions over whether or not women should be ordained as ministers, rabbis, and priests. Such controversy, and the ensuing skepticism that many people have toward clergywomen today, has the potential either to stifle or to spur political activity among women of the cloth.

As their numbers grow, women clergy are coming to exert an increasingly visible presence in American politics. The political significance of women's presence in the pulpit should only be expected to increase in decades to come, particularly in light of the so-called "gender gap" that appears to be separating the politics of men and women in the United States.[11] Gender divisions among mainline Protestant clergy exemplify a broader trend within American society as mainline clergywomen embrace a more left-leaning, feminist approach to politics than their male counterparts.[12] James Davison Hunter and Kimon Howland Sargeant have argued that as more women enter the ministry, mainline Protestantism itself may be pushed even further to the left politically, which could aggravate the culture wars that are said to be raging in the United States over disputes about the meaning of morality.[13]

This book explores the effects of religion and gender on women clergy's political attitudes and actions. We combine qualitative insights from in-depth interviews with women clergy in four different American cities—Omaha, Nebraska; Milwaukee, Wisconsin; Indianapolis, Indiana; and Washington, D.C.—and quantitative analysis of data from a national survey to probe beyond simplistic but common stereotypes that portray clergywomen as either a silent, oppressed minority or the cutting edge of a feminist revolution within American religion. To be sure, women ministers and rabbis face special professional and political constraints on account of their gender. The de facto minority status of women clergy is exacerbated by longstanding religious norms about appropriate gender roles, which often have been used to challenge the ordination and acceptance of women clergy. Women clergy frequently choose or are appointed to relatively low-prestige positions,[14] and some argue that they lack religious authority and respect.[15] They are also more likely than men to leave the ministry.[16] Nevertheless, under some circumstances gender can be a political asset for women in the ministry and rabbinate. This book examines both the constraints and opportunities that women clergy encounter in terms of their willingness and ability to participate in politics. Their gender and religious experiences are keys to understanding their political behavior. Women clergy are unique in that they work in the only American profession to deal explicitly and primarily with the spiritual and the eternal. We consider how both their minority professional status and their personal religious beliefs might shape their political attitudes and behavior.

Women Clergy: Past and Present

Although women from Anne Hutchinson to Frances Willard championed women's rightful place in America's pulpits, organized religion did not begin widespread debate about women's ordination until the twentieth century.[17] Nevertheless, a significant number of women in the nineteenth century were itinerant evangelists, and a few American religious traditions including the Society of Friends (Quakers) and the Universalists allowed women to occupy formal leadership positions. The Disciples of Christ and the Congregationalists also voted to ordain women in the nineteenth century. The first two formally ordained women clergy in the United States were Antoinette Brown, who was ordained by the Congregationalists in 1853, and Olympia Brown, ordained by the Universalists in 1863.[18] Lucretia Mott, the noted suffragist, was also a Quaker preacher.

At roughly the same time, pioneers in the struggle for women's greater societal equality met at the Women's Rights Convention in Seneca Falls. This meeting was, in part, an outgrowth of the abolitionist cause—one of the first social movements in the United States in which it was acceptable for women to take an active leadership role. Many abolitionists, including William Lloyd Garrison, began to link the cause of slaves and women together.[19] Nancy McGlen and her colleagues write that the principal result of the Women's Rights Convention, the Seneca Falls Declaration, reflected women's dissatisfaction with contemporary moral codes, divorce and criminal laws, and limited opportunities for women to obtain an education, participate in the church, and enter careers in medicine, law, and politics.[20] American society, however, failed to embrace the declaration at the time because of its radical, comprehensive nature. Women leaders instead began to focus on gaining the right to vote: a controversial goal that ironically drew more support than the declaration's other, less controversial demands. Suffragists were a mix of liberal and conservative women, many of whom came from the Temperance Movement. Their cause was helped by conservative women leaders, who argued that granting women the right to vote would allow women's moral influence, particularly that of mothers and homemakers, to remedy governmental and societal corruption.[21] Yet restricting the focus of the women's movement to suffrage meant that any attempts to broaden women's employment opportunities, including those involving the pulpit, were largely ignored.

The twentieth century, however, finally brought the battle over women's ordination to its boiling point. In 1948, the African Methodist Episcopal (AME) Church agreed to ordain women, followed in 1954 by the Christian Methodist Episcopal (CME) Church. In 1956, United (northern) Presbyterians and United Methodists followed suit. The Presbyterian Church in the United States (southern Presbyterians) voted to ordain women in 1964.[22] The new women's movement that dawned in the 1960s dramatically raised the stakes for the holdout mainline Protestant denominations. Women were suddenly demanding full social equality, and their desire to have access to the pulpit was but one manifestation of the broader aims of the movement. In 1968, Mary Daly published her devastating *The Church and the Second Sex* (in the mold of Betty Friedan's *The Feminine Mystique*), which was a clarion call for feminism to be brought to bear upon organized religion in the United States.[23] In the 1970s, as Mark Chaves argues, large numbers of women began to demand admittance to the ministry for the first time, in part as a direct response to the women's rights movement.[24] It was at this historical moment (1970) that the two most progressive branches of Lutheranism, the American Lutheran Church and the Lutheran Church in America, agreed to ordain women. Sally Priesand became the first American woman rabbi in 1972 when Reform Judaism embraced women's ordination. The Episcopal Church began ordaining women priests in 1976. Finally, Conservative Judaism began adding women to its rabbinate in 1985.[25]

Despite the gains women have made within mainline Protestantism and Judaism, many American religious traditions continue to stand against the ordination of women. Most noteworthy are the Roman Catholic Church and many of the evangelical Protestant traditions that are thriving today in the United States. The Catholic Church has always rejected the idea of opening the priesthood to women, although it did not begin to argue this point vigorously until the 1970s, when the Anglican Church began ordaining women. Today, approximately two-thirds of all American Catholics say they support women's ordination, but the conservative church hierarchy, headed for more than two decades by Pope John Paul II (who vehemently opposes the notion of women priests), remains firmly against the idea.[26] Catholic leaders cite the fact that priests must serve sacramentally in place of Christ, who was male, as well as the fact that none of Christ's twelve disciples was female. In 2001 Pope John Paul II issued a statement ruling the discussion of women's ordination closed. Yet the battle over allowing women access to the priesthood has raged, and will undoubtedly continue to simmer, within Catholic circles. Radical Catholic women's groups such as Womenchurch have led the charge for women's ordination. Some women religious have also gained influence by infusing feminism into American Catholicism, and the desperate American priest shortage has presented increased opportunities for laywomen to play key roles in mass.[27]

Because it is so much more organizationally diverse than the Catholic Church, evangelical Protestantism sends a more mixed message about the ordination of women. A common belief in evangelical circles is that men should assume a "headship" role in religious matters. Women are expected to participate in worship alongside men, but a popular argument drawn from the Epistles is that women are not qualified to teach men about religious matters. Some claim that evangelicals see women's ordination as "a symbol of the liberal world they are trying to define themselves against."[28] Evangelicals place a great value on preserving tradition—which would include barring women from the pulpit—because they are defined in large part by the traditions that they so passionately uphold—including longstanding perceptions of appropriate gender roles.[29] Yet there are some women to be found in evangelical pulpits, particularly in Pentecostal churches.[30] Women are also allowed to preach under some circumstances in African American Baptist churches.

The battles over women's ordination have been, and continue to be, fierce and divisive. Some American religious traditions have already fought these battles, although not all wounds have healed. Other traditions, such as the Southern Baptist Convention (SBC), continue to struggle with the question of whether women ought to be allowed to serve as clergy. In 2000, the SBC passed a resolution opposing women's ordination.[31] Former president Jimmy Carter then broke his lifelong ties with the denomination in large part because of this issue. In announcing his departure from the SBC, Carter said, "I personally feel the Bible says all people are equal in the eyes of God. I personally feel that women should play an absolutely equal role in service of Christ in the church."[32]

Is There Strength in Numbers?

It would be a mistake to assume that women today constitute anything but a small minority of clergy, even within mainline Protestantism. Table 1.1 shows that women make up less than one-fourth of all clergy in the traditions we study here. Nonetheless, the number of women clergy is on the rise in the aggregate. In 1910, only 685 women identified "clergy" as their occupation for the U.S. Bureau of the Census. That number grew tenfold by 1950, when there were 6,824 women clergy in the United States. By 1980, there were 16,408 women clergy, and the 1990 census found a record-breaking 49,984 American clergywomen. Table 1.1 also displays the tremendous growth in the number of women clergy in the past generation. In many of the religious traditions, the number of women clergy has more than doubled since 1986.

Despite the growing feminization of the ministry and rabbinate, the adult experiences of women in a profession that has been dominated historically by males may play an important role in shaping their political attitudes. Some women clergy even see the very act of serving in the profession as a political statement. One woman minister who was interviewed for this study, for example, argues that women have a "special responsibility" to articulate political concerns that especially affect women because women clergy "stand on the shoulders" of those pioneering women who came before them. She states, "When it comes to issues of equality . . . perhaps women clergy do have a particular need to get involved." However, other clergywomen might view their minority status within the profession as a reason *not* to engage in politics. Women clergy's desire to do a good job performing core ministry functions in a

Table 1.1 Numbers and Percentages of Clergywomen in Eight Religious Traditions over Time

	1977	1986	1994	2000
American Baptist Churches	157 (3%)	429 (10%)	712 (12%)	1,032 (13%)[a]
Conservative Judaism	0	5 (1%)	80 (7%)	127 (9%)
Disciples of Christ	388 (9%)	743 (18%)	988 (18%)	1,564 (22%)
Episcopal Church	94 (1%)	796 (6%)	1,394 (12%)	3,482 (20%)
Evangelical Lutheran Church in America	—[b]	—	1,519 (11%)	2,358 (13%)
Presbyterian Church (U.S.A.)	350 (3%)	1,524 (8%)	2,705 (19%)	3,715 (18%)
Reform Judaism	3 (0.2%)	102 (5%)	223 (10%)	346 (14%)
United Methodist Church	319 (2%)	1,891 (9%)	3,003 (15%)	4,370 (17%)

Sources: Constant Jacquet, National Council of Churches (Protestants, 1977 and 1986); Barbara Brown Zikmund, Adair T. Lummis, and Patricia Mei Yin Chang, Hartford Seminary (Protestants, 1994); News sources of religious traditions (Jews; Protestants, 2000). Numbers may not be directly comparable due to differences in measurement criteria among the various sources of data.

Note: Percents represent percentage of clergy in each tradition who are women.

[a]Data for the American Baptist Churches are from 2001.

[b]The ELCA was founded in 1987, so data for 1977 and 1986 are unavailable.

profession that can be all-consuming, coupled with possible resistance from their congregations and communities over their right to serve in the pulpit, might lead some of them to avoid politics in order to protect their legitimacy. As one of our women subjects relates, "It is still true that women have to do a better job than men do, so women tend to spend more time with church activities and might not have as much time to participate in politics."

Women clergy's experience as a minority within their profession is not the only factor affecting their political choices. Their gender is likely to have a strong impact on their politics as well. In the past decade, much has been made about the "gender gap," which suggests that women as a group may be more politically liberal than men in the United States.[33] For example, scholars have noted since the 1980 election that women are consistently more likely to vote for Democratic candidates than Republican candidates.[34] Virginia Sapiro, in particular, argues that the adult socialization of women into specific gendered family roles has a powerful effect on their political attitudes.[35] Thus we expect that women clergy will take more liberal stances on a variety of political issues.

The gender gap also extends to levels of political participation. Men are more likely to participate in most political activities (aside from voting) than women.[36] Political scientists have also found that gender interacts with the work experiences of women to shape political behavior. Kay Lehman Schlozman and colleagues have examined the interaction of gender and work experiences in general and the impact that these interactions have on political participation. They find that men are more likely to work in job settings where they acquire certain skill sets, such as practicing a civic skill on the job or supervising others, that enhance their ability to participate in the political world. Further, Schlozman and colleagues find that while men work longer hours, on average, than women, women have less free time to devote to political activities because they often are burdened with more commitments at home.[37] While it could be argued that women clergy, as well as their male counterparts, engage in the sort of work that could be conducive to political action, especially in terms of civic engagement, women might be more likely to face the time pressures about which Schlozman and colleagues write. Even if women clergy are not burdened at home, they might feel compelled to spend more time on the job than their male colleagues in order to prove their mettle to potentially hostile congregations. A good deal of work also has been done on the experiences of women as elites in other professions, particularly government, business, and the military.[38] The adult experiences women have in a profession that has been dominated historically by one gender—in this instance, the ministry—may also play an important role in shaping their political attitudes. As Rosabeth Moss Kanter has asserted, work environments shape people, and these shaping experiences have political consequences.

The Importance of Studying Clergy

Not only does studying clergywomen offer an opportunity to further our knowledge about how working in a male-dominated profession potentially shapes the political choices of women in one particular profession, it is also important because of the distinctive positions clergy hold within their larger communities. While clergy are paradigmatic of nongovernmental social leaders in that political participation is not their primary responsibility, clergy are in a position where they *may* find politics relevant to their work, particularly if they have a strong sense of themselves as community leaders. At various times throughout American history, clergy have found politics relevant to their ministry, and they have taken visible political roles by speaking out on issues such as abolition, temperance, civil rights, abortion, and international debt relief. Recently, government initiatives have encouraged pastors and their congregations to take more active roles in the provision of social services in their communities. These initiatives range from the well-publicized Charitable Choice provision of federal welfare reform law, which allows religious congregations to compete with secular agencies for federal funding, to efforts by local governments to partner with congregations.[39] Highlighting the important roles that religious organizations (and consequently clergy) may play in public policy, one of President George W. Bush's first actions was to create a White House Office of Faith-based and Community Initiatives.

Clergy do share characteristics with other professionals who find themselves involved in politics in ways that relate to their primary occupation. Yet clergy are also different in that their views and pronouncements carry the force of moral suasion because these individuals represent a social institution (organized religion) that is explicitly designed to provide moral guidance. Generally speaking, clergy are in a unique position to shape the interplay of religion and politics in the United States.

Over half of all Americans say they attend religious services at least once a month.[40] Even if this figure is inflated, as some scholars have argued, Americans indisputably attend religious services far more regularly than citizens of other countries.[41] At least once a week, therefore, American clergy have opportunities to provide political cues through sermons, study groups, and lessons. For the most part, clergy appear to use these opportunities to discuss politics at least on occasion.[42] These cues do not fall on deaf ears, and there is some evidence that clergy pronouncements do affect congregation members' political behavior.[43] Moreover, some clergy participate directly in politics and the policy process.[44] Some bring religious thought and experiences to policy discussions. Others are active in citywide coalitions to address poverty and violence. And it is by no means unreasonable to say that the civil rights movement would never have been born, much less have succeeded, were it not for the political involvement of clergy.[45] Given the large percentage of Americans who attend religious services with at least some regularity, in addition to the fact that clergy who get involved in politics can clearly make a difference, the role of clergy and congregations deserves much more attention in the broader study of organized interests and political mobilization.[46]

Most of the recent work on the political choices of clergy has focused on broad national survey samples and has not incorporated gender as an important analytical element. The first studies of clergy involvement in politics were designed to document and explore the radicalization of mainline Protestant clergy during the civil rights movement.[47] Taken together, these early studies became the benchmark of scholarship on clergy in politics for two decades. Only recently has scholarly attention again been paid to the political involvement of clergy. Both James Guth and colleagues and Paul Djupe and Christopher Gilbert have amassed and analyzed multitudinous surveys on clergy's political beliefs and practices; Ted Jelen and Laura Olson have each embraced a more ethnographic approach by interviewing clergy and visiting their churches.[48] This book extends both research traditions by combining the deep insights that only ethnographic research can offer with the breadth afforded by survey research.

In this book, we focus on the political consequences of the dynamics that affect the types of women who choose to enter the ministry and rabbinate, as well as how the women are socialized into the profession.

We also analyze the shared interests of clergy from mainline Protestant denominations and Reform and Conservative Judaism to determine how such interests shape women clergy's politics. In addition, we recognize and consider how the daily life experiences of women clergy, which include the organizational pressures they face from both their congregations and their denominations, factor into their political choices.

Religion, Gender, and the Politics of Women Clergy

Gender is not the only factor that shapes women clergy's political attitudes and behaviors. We also investigate how women clergy's political activity flows from a sense of divine religious calling, as these women are unique among professionals in that they work in the only American profession to deal specifically with spiritual matters. And we consider how organized religion, via the activities and structures of their religious traditions, shapes clergywomen's political choices.

The cultures of the specific religious traditions that ordain women form the backdrop against which the drama of balancing ministry and political choices plays out. The various elements of these religious contexts have important ramifications for the political drama as well, as they are all typically rooted in a strong social justice tradition. In many mainline Protestant denominations, concern about social justice issues such as poverty and racism is highly consistent with the belief that religious people should be actively involved in the culture, addressing the problems of the less fortunate in a "Christlike" manner.[49] Similar concern about social justice issues among Jews stems from the Jewish people's ongoing struggle for justice and acceptance. One of the rabbis we interviewed remarked that her movement of Judaism is "very strongly committed to social justice issues and trying to follow the words of the prophets" and that she sees this fact as a "guiding principle for all rabbis." The women's personal religious beliefs are likely reinforced by their professional experiences and their gender. For example, seminary attendance may socialize future ministers and rabbis to embrace the political and social goals advocated by their religious traditions. One minister we interviewed explained: "Seminary gave me more of an understanding of justice and a need to work towards that understanding."

While we argue that gender, minority professional status, and the nature of the religious traditions that support female ordination all push clergywomen toward the political left, these same factors can combine to make it difficult and potentially risky for women clergy to engage in visible action on controversial issues, especially those of a stereotypically liberal ilk. Despite the relatively liberal nature of the official social teachings and traditions of the denominations in which these women work, congregations often hold more conservative views.[50] There are many good reasons to expect women clergy to avoid politics in order to protect their legitimacy. The ways in which they negotiate their political choices in this complex professional context emerge as a fascinating component of the stories of their political lives.

Studying patterns in the political mobilization of women clergy helps to elucidate the broader phenomena of the choices that elites in nongovernmental realms make about political involvement, as well as the constraints women in any context must overcome in order to influence American political discourse. The fact that women clergy must make political choices in a professional setting in which they are clearly a minority, and in which their minority status may be intensified by traditional religious norms about appropriate gender roles, makes analysis of their political choices all the more interesting and important.

2
The Components of Clergywomen's Political Mobilization

It is not rare to find clergywomen taking part in the political sphere both inside and outside of their congregations. Within the four walls of their congregations' houses of worship, clergywomen may take part in political discussions that bubble up in congregational study groups, or they may comment formally on political matters from the pulpit. Quite often, however, women clergy enter the political sphere in ways that take them into the world beyond their congregations.

In light of the fact that women clergy's political activities can take so many forms, it is incumbent upon us to state what we mean by *political activity*. There are multitudinous definitions of politics, and consequently an enormous variety of ways to identify what sorts of actions count as political activity. Most definitions of politics focus on the process through which communities make collective decisions about the proper distribution of resources, the bounds of shared values, or appropriate standards of behavior.[1] In this spirit, we accept *political activities* to mean actions taken to influence collective decision-making processes concerning resource distribution or the development and enforcement of shared values.

Scholars of political participation traditionally have devoted most of their attention to people's participation in elections and partisan politics.[2] These studies focus primarily on the processes by which individuals are selected to fill government positions and make collective decisions for the community, processes that are indisputably major components of politics. However, much of the political activity in which women clergy engage falls outside the bounds of this circumscribed set of political activities. Instead of being primarily electoral or partisan, their political work often involves activities that focus on pursuing changes in resource distribution or behavior in relation to particular issues. Some endeavor to change rules concerning gay marriage, others to reduce racism, and still others to secure resources for homeless people. At times this sort of political engagement occurs naturally as clergy work in their local communities to resolve public problems such as gang violence and drug abuse. At other times their issue-oriented activism is a reaction to a government decision or debate. For example, in early 2003 many clergy engaged in antiwar activism in reaction against the United States' invasion of Iraq. They contacted public officials, joined coalitions to push for a different foreign policy, and organized rallies and conferences to educate others about the issue.

Clergy's engagement in collective decision making is also facilitated by partnerships with government agencies. For instance, a minister or rabbi may participate in a state-funded job-training program or join a local government-sponsored coalition to fight racism in the community. Such partnerships have garnered increasing public attention as more and more politicians and nonprofit entrepreneurs work to develop faith-based initiatives to address policy problems.[3] This issue activism can even include efforts by nongovernmental organizations, such as religious congregations, to address public problems without government support.

The process of politics, then, runs from the election of governmental leaders down to the nuts and bolts of running programs and solving common problems on the ground. Political activity comprises the myriad ways in which ordinary citizens enter and affect the processes through which collective decisions are made and carried out. This understanding of politics pushes the definition of political activities beyond the typical electoral and partisan foci of many traditional studies of political mobilization in two ways.[4] First, we include involvement in the *implementation* of policy as political activity. Much of the current interest in faith-based initiatives focuses on how religious leaders and organizations participate in implementation activities. Second, we include collective attempts to influence resource distribution and behavior in one's community that occur even when government is not involved in any significant way. Since this latter expansion could include nearly any activity, we narrow the scope to encompass only activities that lead clergy to reach beyond the bounds of their congregations. To illustrate: working with a coalition of clergy and other community leaders to establish a food bank would count, whereas urging church elders to take food to a hungry family in the congregation would not.

Our analysis of women clergy's political work focuses primarily on two dimensions of their political activities: the nature of the political *issues* upon which women clergy act (such as abortion, homelessness, or education) and the political *strategies* that they employ to achieve their goals (such as campaigning, government partnership, or direct service). Throughout the book we examine how religion and gender influence clergywomen's political principles and priorities—and how religion and gender each shape the ways in which clergywomen translate their political principles and priorities into political action. As we argue throughout the book, most of these women's political principles and priorities fit squarely into a social justice mission. As scholars of political mobilization, we are most interested in how this mission gets translated into political action. How do pressures from religious institutions (both positive and negative) shape clergywomen's political actions? How do clergywomen adjust their actions to fit their interpretation of contemporary political circumstances? How are they recruited for political activity, and how do they respond to such invitations?

Sources of Data: The Women Clergy We Study

In order to make sense of the political priorities and political actions of women clergy, we spent many hours speaking with fifty-four women clergy in four cities (Milwaukee, Indianapolis, Omaha, and Washington, D.C.) during the spring and summer of 1998. These women include ministers who serve in six mainline Protestant denominations—the American Baptist Churches, the Christian Church (Disciples of Christ), the Episcopal Church, the Evangelical Lutheran Church in America, the Presbyterian Church (U.S.A.), and the United Methodist Church—as well as Reform and Conservative rabbis. Using a stratified sample to ensure diversity among religious traditions, we chose interviewees' names at random from lists provided by each religious tradition.[5] Our sample is small, but so too is the population from which it was drawn. In fact, the sample includes over two-thirds of the population of women clergy serving in mainline Protestant and Jewish traditions in these four cities. Four of the women are African American (but do not serve in traditionally African American denominations). The clergy we contacted were very interested in talking about their experiences, resulting in an excellent response rate of 87 percent.[6]

At the end of each interview we asked the minister or rabbi to complete a short survey. The survey allowed us to focus our interview time on questions that were best suited to in-depth, qualitative measurement. The survey also included questions that match those regularly used in national studies of clergy. A new round of national clergy studies in 2000 (undertaken under the auspices of the Cooperative Clergy Project, organized by Corwin Smidt of Calvin College) used many of these same questions, allowing us to compare results from some of the questions asked of the women we interviewed to results from a national random sample of clergywomen. The Cooperative Clergy Project involved twenty clergy scholars, including the authors of this book, who created a shared survey instrument and sent it to random samples of clergy in different religious traditions immediately following the 2000 presidential election. The resulting national database contains many thousands of clergy who serve in a wide variety of religious traditions, including all but one of the traditions (the Episcopal Church) covered by our 1998 interviews.[7] The juxtaposition of our interview and survey work in four cities and these national data provides an opportunity to explore the rich community-grounded stories of the political choices of women with the rare advantage of being able to assess the generalizability of these insights. In nearly every chapter we compare the urban women we interviewed with the picture of clergywomen generated by the 2000 Cooperative Clergy Project. In most cases, the two pictures are similar. Where the pictures differ, an interesting story lurks in the background. The availability of the national data also allows us to test for statistical patterns in the choices of women clergy with a level of sophistication that would not be possible with data from only fifty-four women.

We interviewed and collected surveys from most of the mainline Protestant and Jewish women clergy in each of our four target cities.

Why did we focus on just mainline Protestants and Jews? Many American religious traditions, especially the Roman Catholic Church and most of evangelical Protestantism, do not ordain women to pulpit ministries. Other traditions, such as Pentecostalism and African American Protestantism, have no consistent or predictable pattern of allowing women formal access to the ministry.[8] The Cooperative Clergy Project, which examined random samples of clergy from many different religious traditions, confirms that very few women show up on clergy lists for faith groups outside of mainline Protestantism and Judaism in the United States. The largest numbers of women outside of the mainline and Jewish traditions were found for the Assemblies of God (6 percent) and the Church of the Nazarene (3 percent), with women clergy being the rare exception in each. All other evangelical and Pentecostal traditions yielded even fewer women (1 percent or less). We therefore focus solely on traditions with longstanding and formalized traditions of women's ordination and with larger numbers of women clergy: mainline Protestantism and Reform and Conservative Judaism.[9] Our focus on mainline Protestant and Jewish women clergy also enables us to examine clergy who work in traditions with long histories of political activism and, especially for mainline Protestant women, political tension. Critics might charge that our focus on mainline Protestantism and Judaism is ill placed due to the numerical declines in both traditions in recent decades.[10] Despite these losses, however, both traditions remain strong forces in American religious, social, and political culture, and neither shows signs of vanishing anytime soon.[11]

We chose the four cities primarily because they were cities that we understood politically. Each of us had conducted previous extensive political research in one of three of the cities (Milwaukee, Indianapolis, and Washington, D.C.).[12] Each city was also familiar to one of us because we had lived in or near it for a time. Our familiarity with these four cities allowed us a long view of the context in which these clergywomen choose their political priorities and make decisions about how to act politically. The four-city focus also made it possible for us to use news sources and similarities that emerged in the interviews in each city to understand major issues and events in that city so that the information we collected from the ministers and rabbis could be put into context. The four cities provide a mix of midwestern cities and a contrast in the form of a large, east coast metropolitan area. The cities also provide a good variety of political contexts; two of the cities are rooted primarily in conservative politics (Omaha and Indianapolis), and two tend toward more liberal politics (Milwaukee and Washington, D.C.). The interviews, then, combined with our own extensive knowledge of the cities, furnish rich accounts of the ways in which these ministers and rabbis interpret their mission—and translate that mission into action in the specific time and place that they find themselves.

Our aim for this book, however, is to go beyond the details of the women's stories to uncover patterns that illustrate how gender and religion work to shape the political views and actions of these women clergy. Our objective is to provide a grounded understanding of the mission and politics of female ministers and rabbis, which offers broader insights into the interplay of politics, religion, and gender. Although our focus in this book stays firmly on clergywomen, we have consistently argued that the methods and theories developed from our studies of these women may fruitfully be applied to studies of the politics of other professional groups.[13]

All of the women in our four-city study and all of the women in the national survey studies hold congregational positions. Women clergy working exclusively in mission, counseling, or social ministry positions are not included. This means that some of the most politically active women clergy may have been excluded, as those who wish to involve themselves heavily in political action have been shown to prefer noncongregational positions.[14] However, the women in noncongregational positions are excluded so as to focus on the political decisions of those who are forced to balance political involvement with the substantial responsibility of serving a congregation.

In terms of basic demographic and political characteristics, the clergy in the four cities look a lot like the national samples of women clergy (in the same traditions) who answered the Cooperative Clergy Project survey. As the first three rows in table 2.1 illustrate, both samples yield a picture of clergywomen as highly interested in politics, ideologically left leaning, and quite Democratic in their party affiliation. The four-city women stand out as identifying even more strongly with a liberal ideology. Throughout the book we explore whether this ideological difference results in any distinct differences in the political choices of these urban women. The demographic similarities between the two groups are striking. The two sets of women match very closely in terms of age, marital status, race, and education. The ministry and congregational experiences of the two samples also match well. The four-city women and the women in the national study have similar tenures in the ministry and in their present congregations. The main difference here is the larger average size of the congregations that the four-city women serve, but even these differences are not dramatic. It makes sense that urban congregations would tend to be slightly larger than those of a national sample that includes rural and small-town churches along with urban and suburban churches. Overall, table 2.1 shows that the women's political similarities (in terms of their high level of political interest and overwhelmingly liberal ideology and Democratic party identification) and their demographic similarities far outweigh any differences.

The national Cooperative Clergy Project survey includes clergywomen from all of the traditions that we cover in our study except Episcopalians. The denominational ratios differ between the two samples, but this is less important than shared political and demographic characteristics, since we focus throughout on the common religious heritage and experiences of these women. Although denominational organizations play key roles in the mobilization of many of these women, few differences between religious traditions emerge as politically important in our analysis.

Mapping the Analysis

We began this study with the conviction that there was much to be learned about religion, politics, and gender from clergywomen. We also shared an intellectual interest in how the political contexts in which people work serve to shape their political views and actions. Studies, including some of our own, have shown a variety of ways in which workplace dynamics shape political choices and politicize gender differences.[15] As we review in chapter 1, there is good reason to expect workplace dynamics for mainline Protestant and Jewish women clergy to be fertile ground for political mobilization. But we may also very well find

Table 2.1 Demographic Comparison of Four-City and National Samples

Characteristic	Four-City Sample	National Sample
Interest in politics	79%	75%
Liberal political ideology	80%	69%
Democratic Party affiliation	71%	75%
Average age	45	48
Married	69%	65%
White	92%	94%
Seminary graduate	92%	96%
Average years in ministry	13	12
Average years in current congregation	5	5
Average adult members	638	419
Average weekly attendance	242	191
Religious Tradition		
American Baptist Churches	11%	6%
Disciples of Christ	9%	18%
Episcopal Church	11%	—
Evangelical Lutheran Church in America	11%	20%
Jewish traditions	11%	15%
Presbyterian Church (U.S.A.)	19%	12%
United Methodist Church	28%	44%*

Sources: Compiled by authors from interviews; Cooperative Clergy Project 2000.
*The United Methodist sample includes an over-sample of women clergy.

pressures within their religious traditions and congregations that discourage political activity, especially among women.

To set the stage for our exploration of clergywomen's political choices, chapter 3 will provide a look at the shared religious heritage of these women. We emphasize their common social justice mission and their interpretations of how their gender shapes their application of this mission. As chapter 3 illustrates, the women's shared social justice mission yields some widely shared political worldviews. In addition to their similar political views, the women also share work experiences in common. And as table 2.1 shows, they also largely share important demographic characteristics.

The relative homogeneity of these women raises challenges for analysis. Statistical analysis of political choices usually focuses on explaining *differences*. For example, a statistical model can determine which variables best explain why some people are more likely than others to contribute to political campaigns. If the model shows that income and party affiliation best explain these differences, then we argue that income and party affiliation help to explain why people give campaign contributions. In other words, we usually explain political mobilization by understanding *differences between* the subjects in our studies. Because we were all trained in this kind of analysis, we began our study of women clergy by trying to understand their political choices by examining differences that might distinguish them from each other. And despite the women's homogeneity, this sort of analysis does provide some important insights. In chapter 5 we employ it to understand the differences between women who take political action to address the issues that concern them most and those who do not display such consistency. In chapter 6 we use a similar approach to understand differences between women who employ different political strategies.

However, our efforts to understand how these women become politically mobilized have convinced us that there is at least as much to be learned from the striking *similarities* among these women. There is, for instance, more to be learned from exploring why nearly all of the clergywomen we interviewed see themselves as political liberals than there is from analysis that compares the most liberal women to the moderately liberal. Statistics offer little help for understanding similarities, since they explain variance. Instead we turn to qualitative analysis of these women's own experiences, in conjunction with insights from the histories of their religious traditions and the gender experiences of women in the ministry and rabbinate, to interpret the political implications of the similarities we find among clergywomen. Chapter 3 focuses most extensively on this analysis by emphasizing the women's shared religious traditions and gender experiences. Each succeeding chapter also examines what we can learn from the women's shared experiences and choices.

Since we do focus on a rather homogeneous group, we can put aside some standard analyses of political mobilization. There is little need to explore socioeconomic differences within this group of almost all white, highly educated women.[16] The dominance of Democratic Party allegiance suggests that party affiliation is also unlikely to explain political differences among these women. Similarly, we would expect little to be gained from analyses of religious beliefs due to the strong homogeneity the women evince on this dimension. These clergywomen hail from denominations or traditions that fully embrace what James Guth and colleagues term a "communitarian" social theology, which is grounded in a liberal interpretation of religious text.[17] For instance, 81 percent of women in the national sample agree or strongly agree with the statement "Social justice is at the heart of the gospel." Additionally, almost three-fourths of the women in our four-city sample self-describe their theology as radical, very liberal, or somewhat liberal.

Existing general political theories that stress issue interests, organizational pressures (including work organizations), recruitment, and political contexts offer a more fruitful way to analyze political mobilization among these clergywomen.[18] Studies of clergy activism confirm that these theoretical arguments often hold among clergy.[19] Our political analysis of clergywomen constantly comes back to three basic questions about their political mobilization: About which political issues do they care most? On which political issues do they act? And which political strategies do they use when they do act? We refer to the issues that concern clergywomen most as their *political priorities*. Chapter 4 provides a picture of the political priorities of the four-city women and compares their priorities to those that emerge from the national sample. Analyzing the issues that most concern these women allows us to glimpse how religion and gender experiences work to shape the women's political worldview. This analysis fits a longstanding emphasis in public opinion studies of discerning public views of the "most important problems." In chapter 4 we take advantage of public opinion polling to compare the political priorities of clergywomen to those of the public at large.

Assessment of political priorities also provides clues as to the types of issues around which these clergywomen might be mobilized to act. However, as we discuss in chapter 5, there are myriad reasons why clergy may not end up focusing their political action on the issues that personally concern them. When clergywomen act politically, upon what issues are they most likely to act? We refer to this set of issues on which clergy act as their *action agendas*.[20] We use information about the political activities clergywomen undertake to determine the extent to which they act to address specific political issues, such as gay rights, abortion, or poverty. Chapter 5 shows the issue distribution of their political actions and explores how their action agendas make sense in terms of their religious and gender experiences.

Because we know the nature of the women's political priorities, and we know which issues tend to inform their political actions, we can turn to the question of whether their priorities *match* their action agendas. Why might some women take action primarily to address their own priorities, whereas others do not do so? In chapter 5 we examine how religious influences and gender experiences shape these consistencies and inconsistencies with particular attention to theories of issue mobilization (the idea that people are mobilized to act based on their own personal passion for an issue), organizational mobilization (which posits that people are mobilized to act because of organizational pressures), and recruitment (people act because others ask them to do so).

Regardless of the issue foci of their political activities, clergywomen who wish to enter the political fray must choose some means by which to do so. We refer to the specific ways in which clergywomen engage in politics as their *political strategies*. As our definition of politics makes clear, we recognize a broad set of options as viable political strategies. A clergywoman may implement these strategies either within her congregation or in the world beyond her church or synagogue. Chapter 6 outlines the frequency with which clergywomen use a variety of political strategies, from giving political cues in sermons to political campaigning, and from working with a local advocacy group to partnering with government to tackle some local problem. Chapter 6 draws upon both qualitative and quantitative data to answer key questions about the women's political strategies. Why do they choose specific strategies? How do their choices make sense in light of their religious and gender experiences?

Chapters 4, 5, and 6, then, focus on analysis of three key political variables: political priorities (chapter 4), action agendas (chapter 5), and political strategies (chapter 6). In each of these chapters we analyze the influence of religion and gender using both qualitative and quantitative data. Throughout, we integrate our analyses of religion, gender, and political mobilization by focusing on two primary pathways: the development of political *principles* and religious *organizational pressures*. The twin influences of political principles and religious institutions, however, do not operate in isolation. The realities of everyday *politics*—including the public agenda, existing policy, the mix of political leaders in place, and key political organizations—also mold political mobilization. This final category, politics, may also include the effect of elites that the clergywomen encounter outside of their religious traditions (for example, a rabbi might receive an invitation from the mayor to join a task force on race relations). Our analysis of each of the three products of political mobilization (priorities, action agendas, and political strategies) examines how principles and organizational pressures interact with external political dynamics. We use these three constructs (principles, organizational pressures, and politics) to understand the clergywomen's political priorities and political actions in ways that build on existing theories of political mobilization.

Figure 2.1 maps out the relationships among the three theoretical constructs and the three products of political mobilization into a basic framework that guides our analysis throughout the book.[21] The figure also indicates which chapters address each part of the framework. The basic gist of the theoretical framework is that religion and gender shape both the women's political principles and the organizational pressures they face. These personal principles and organizational pressures in turn combine with the political contexts in which the women live and work to shape their political priorities, their issue agendas, and their political strategies.

Principles, organizational pressures, and politics influence the extent to which clergywomen take action to address the issues that concern them most and the ways in which they may gravitate toward action on issues that do not rank among their top personal concerns. Similarly, the women choose political strategies that will fit their principles, mesh with the organizational pressures they face, and work within their political context. Although we focus on religion and gender primarily as they affect principles and organizational pressures (as pictured in figure 2.1), we discuss other ways in which religion and gender enter political calcula-

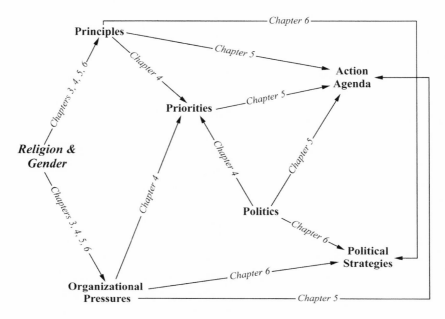

Figure 2.1. Political Mobilization Framework

tions. Some women talk about how either their religious background or their gender makes them more likely to be recruited for political activities, which would be examples of religion or gender working through politics.

Principles

Principles form the normative foundation for political action. They establish why someone should get involved in politics, what kinds of actions are appropriate or inappropriate, and the larger goals of political involvement. When we look for clergywomen's principles, we look for evidence that these women rely upon norms when assessing when and how to engage in politics. Of greatest interest in this regard are ways in which religion and gender experiences have internalized or strengthened particular political norms. The women's shared social justice mission that we introduce in chapter 1 and explain in more detail in chapter 3 establishes a widely shared set of basic normative principles about the proper purpose and scope of politics. We see these norms emerge in our analyses of the women's political choices again and again in chapters 4, 5, and 6. The political principles that arise from the social justice mission are one of the key similarities that must be understood to make sense of the politics of clergywomen.

Our category of principles includes political attitudes that are often described as components of political ideology. These include interpretations of political values such as justice and liberty, and beliefs about which political values should be given priority. Table 2.1 shows that these women largely identify themselves as political liberals. Previous studies of the political ideology of clergywomen confirm this strong liberal orientation; clergywomen hold distinctly more liberal attitudes than their male colleagues from the same theologically liberal religious traditions.[22] Past studies have also revealed a strong feminist orientation among a large portion of clergywomen. Barbara Brown Zikmund and her colleagues report that over half of the clergywomen in their study express strong feminist convictions concerning denominational and spiritual matters.[23] Similarly, we find a strong feminist bent in the political principles of many of the women in our studies. In chapters 3 and 4 we look more closely at how these women explain and interpret their liberal and feminist views (or in some cases, their rejection of feminism). Of particular interest are ways in which liberal and feminist views are established and reinforced by socialization in the women's religious traditions, by their gender experiences in seminary, and by the male-dominated clerical profession in which they work. How do the sacred texts and teachings of the women's religious traditions shape their views? To what extent do their experiences in seminary and in the profession matter?

Political principles, particularly for women in a profession that stresses morality, include more than just ideology. They also include religious and professional norms concerning the specific types of political strategies that are either appropriate or inappropriate and the nature of the political issues that must or must not be tackled. For example, previous studies of clergy point to a shared norm among many mainline clergy that spiritual leaders should not behave in partisan ways, especially in their roles as religious leaders of the congregation.[24] Nevertheless, concerns about partisanship among these clergy do not prevent them from acting or speaking on specific political issues.[25] Chapter 3 includes analysis of ways in which clergy draw from their religious traditions in attempting to strike an appropriate balance between prescriptions to preach about and work for justice with the imperative of avoiding the appearance of being inappropriately political. Chapter 6 examines the ways in which clergy-women establish principles concerning specific political strategies that guide them in striking this balance.

One other source of political principles that is rarely examined, even in studies of religion and politics, is the notion of divine calling. Do clergy see their divine callings as relevant to politics? Chapter 3 explores this question and reports the extent to which clergywomen feel that they are compelled by a divine calling to enter the political realm. Those who perceive a divine calling either to speak about politics or to act politically have amidst their mix of principles a strong religious norm that empha-sizes the appropriateness of political action. On the other hand, divine callings may establish a religious principle for a minister or rabbi that politics must only be pursued if it does not distract from other, more central divine callings. As chapter 3 reports, we find much more evidence of callings that encourage political action among these women.

Organizational Pressures

To focus more clearly on the impact of religious institutions and work-place dynamics, we combine the organizational pressures that emanate from congregations and those that spring from religious traditions at large in our "organizational pressure" category. We examine organiza-tional pressures that do not come from *religious* organizations in our analysis of *external* political dynamics. In this sense our definition of or-ganizational pressure is narrower than that described by Steven Rosen-stone and John Mark Hansen, as well as that used by scholars who apply Rosenstone and Hansen's theory to clergy under the rubric "organiza-tional mobilization."[26] However, this narrower distinction helps us iso-late the effects of the religious workplace from the influences of other aspects of the political environment for clergywomen. Chapters 4, 5, and 6 all discuss influences of religious institutions by examining the various ways that organizational pressures manifest themselves in the clergy-women's political attitudes and behaviors. Our definition of organizational pressures includes organizational mobilization that comes from congregation members or other organizations that are integral to the women's religious traditions, such as denominational advocacy groups or social service agencies. A rabbi who leads a congregation with a long-standing tradition of having a socially active rabbi may well face congregational pressure to continue that tradition. A Disciples of Christ minister may be encouraged to establish a study group in her congregation on racism because of the high-profile racial reconciliation initiative in her denomination. Chapter 3 includes accounts in which clergy-women explain how this kind of positive organizational mobilization occurs within their religious institutions. Chapters 5 and 6 examine the ways in which the priorities and activities of the women's religious institutions manifest themselves in the action agendas and political strategies the women choose for themselves.

Our analysis of organizational pressures, however, takes a broader form than most analyses of organizational mobilization in that we also examine the flip side of organizational mobilization to assess the ways in which these same religious organizations may generate negative pressures that discourage political activity. Our analysis of organizational pressures includes attention to organizational mobilization and organizational *demobilization*. Much attention in studies of clergy activism has been given to the demobilizing effect that results from friction created by political differences between liberal mainline clergy and the conservative mainline laity in the pews (the clergy-laity gap).[27] Chapters 5 and 6 examine the extent to which we see the clergy-laity gap acting as a demobilizing pressure for these women and explore other demobilizing organizational pressures generated by their religious institutions.

Another form of organizational pressure that clergy encounter is the need for the congregation to survive and (ideally) thrive. Pressure to focus on congregational growth can take attention away from politics. However, past studies show that this pressure can push clergy, especially those in the social justice tradition, toward enhanced activism. Some clergy in these traditions assume that their congregations will benefit, not lose, from their participation in community development and service delivery.[28] Clergy stress the direct benefits that flow from the enhanced visibility of their congregations and the increased opportunities that their members receive to live out their faith. They also identify indirect benefits for the neighborhoods surrounding their congregations, which in turn affect the viability of the congregation.[29]

The pressures that religious organizations exert on these women, combined with the consuming nature of the ministry and rabbinate, also place tremendous time pressures on these women. This time crunch constitutes another form of organizational pressure—and another source of similarity among women clergy. Political activity must either fit into their ministry routines or take a back seat to their primary ministry responsibilities.[30] Chapters 5 and 6 explore ways in which the clergy-women's action agendas and political strategies reveal their efforts to fit political actions into their ministry routines. Time pressures can also increase the impact of politics on the mobilization of these women. Clergy are usually too busy to spend considerable time searching for opportunities to participate in political activities. Consequently, their action choices are shaped by the nature of the opportunities that somehow come their way, which in turn depends to a great extent on political context.

Chapters 4, 5, and 6 all discuss influences of religious institutions by examining the various ways in which organizational pressures manifest themselves in the political attitudes and behaviors of clergywomen. Together with chapter 3, these chapters also examine how clergywomen see their gender intensifying or reducing organizational pressures. At the start of this project, we expected the minority professional status of these women to exacerbate their sensitivity to organizational pressures.[31] We reasoned that women clergy, entering positions previously filled predominantly by males, would be additionally sensitive to organizational pressures to conform, and would wish to avoid appearing too strongly feminist. Past studies had shown that women clergy often feel that their professional legitimacy and authority are threatened because of their gender.[32] It made sense to expect that women clergy would therefore wish to avoid adding fuel to the fire by acting on issues that might be seen as controversial by their congregations or their superiors, or by engaging in political strategies that are either visible or partisan or both. Thus, we expected that organizational demobilizing pressures would be reinforced by gender concerns. However, the analysis that unfolds in the following chapters reveals a richer and more complex story of the ways in which these women perceive and react to organizational pressures.

Politics

Politics can focus clergywomen's attention on particular public problems or policies. For example, one woman explained that a recent rash of murders in her community had focused her political attention and energy (her priorities and action agenda) on efforts to reduce violence. The following chapters include several accounts from women who explain how they chose their priorities or their actions in response to policy decisions in their communities, such as welfare reform and school choice policies.

Political realities also structure the constrained set of opportunities available to clergywomen to become involved in politics. One of the surest paths to political involvement is to be asked by someone else to become involved.[33] It is well established that recruitment is a strong force in political mobilization, and busy women clergy should be no different than anyone else on that front. The politics that shape the larger community help determine who is likely to recruit women clergy for political activity, which in turn shapes the set of issues on which these women clergy have a chance to act. How do minority professional status and gender itself impact this recruitment? Are women clergy unlikely to be recruited into the broader politics of the community, or might their minority professional status instead make them attractive recruits?

The nature of politics in the community at a specific point in time will influence the sorts of political tasks that clergy might be recruited to undertake as well as the opportunities that clergy who seek political outlets might encounter. Recent changes in federal law have made it easier for religious organizations to contract for social services. The Charitable Choice provision of current welfare law now allows congregations to compete for federal funding. It also allows state governments to partner with congregations to provide social services using federal funds.[34] This legal provision, combined with the current positive political attention to faith-based initiatives, opens the door for greater participation by clergy in partnership efforts with government.

Local politics clearly matter here as well. A rabbi in a city whose mayor is committed to partnering with congregations will have a much easier time adopting such a strategy than will a minister in another city where the mayor strongly opposes ties between church and state. And local politics structure the set of issues on which clergy act. It is easier to get involved in work to improve race relations in a city where numerous racism coalitions are already up and running, for example.

Conclusion

Social justice principles emphasize the importance of working to alleviate poverty, to change social structures, to reduce discrimination, and to decrease violence. The political priorities that a minister or rabbi embraces are very frequently rooted in these principles, which guide her toward the specific set of current issues that ought to concern her most at any particular point. Some clergy maintain a consistent set of priorities over the course of their careers, whereas others shift their priorities to fit changes in organizational pressures or politics.

Of most importance in the end is the translation of social justice–related political priorities and principles into political actions. Which issues do clergywomen tackle? Which political strategies do they choose? These questions take us to the far right-hand side of figure 2.1, and full circle in this chapter's discussion of the political mobilization framework. The rest of the book turns to analyses of principles, organizational pressures, and politics in order to answer our central political mobilization questions: Why do these women take political action on some political issues more than on others? Why do they choose specific sorts of political strategies when they take action? And how do religion and gender structure these political choices?

3
Religion, Gender, and the Social Justice Mission

Clergywomen's workaday worlds have ramifications for their encounters with politics. Yet the ministry and rabbinate are not professions like all others; being a clergyperson means working in a distinct realm of society that deals explicitly with spiritual matters. How do the religious dimensions of clergywomen's lives affect the political dimensions of their lives? The religious traditions that ordain women share a longstanding social justice mission that is likely to resonate even more powerfully for clergywomen, who sometimes struggle for acceptance in a role traditionally filled by men. Women clergy's shared encounters with the various manifestations of religious life may mean that they translate their religious callings, beliefs, and experiences into common political principles, action agendas, and political strategies. In this chapter, we emphasize the similarities that link women clergy. We examine religious bases for their political action by focusing first on their internal, personal sense of religious calling. We then examine how the women are affected by external, organizational manifestations of religion: the denominations, movements, and congregations in which they serve. Finally, we study how gender itself affects women clergy's propensity to become involved in politics across different religious traditions. Do specific religious traditions create different atmospheres for women?

It goes without saying that religion is a multifaceted sociocultural phenomenon. Émile Durkheim defines religion as "a unified system of beliefs and practices relative to sacred things, . . . which unite into one single moral community, called a church, all those who adhere to them."[1]

Religion manifests itself in countless ways in both individual and collective life. The internal dimensions of religion variously lead individuals to pray, to worship, and to embrace specific moral codes that guide their behavior. Collectively, religion plays both unifying and divisive roles, at once bringing together individuals who share a common belief system and creating divisions between and among groups on the basis of religious beliefs and practices. Thus religion affects the individual dimension of internal spirituality as well as the group phenomenon of religious institutionalization. Clergy's political lives must therefore be shaped by both their internal, personal spirituality and their religious traditions' external organizational structures.

Religion, broadly construed, involves the drawing of distinctions between the sacred and the profane. As Durkheim argues, "Sacred things are things protected and isolated by prohibitions; profane things are those things to which the prohibitions are applied and that must keep at a distance from what is sacred. Religious beliefs are those representations that express the nature of sacred things and the relations they have with other sacred things or with profane things."[2] The work that clergy do places them in contact with both the sacred and the profane (or secular). In leading worship services and praying with congregation members, for instance, they operate primarily in the realm of the sacred. When they engage in community work outside of the walls of the church or synagogue, however, one might argue that they enter into the realm of the secular—albeit in an effort to infuse a "fallen" world with God's forgiving love. Mainline Protestantism and Judaism in particular do not enforce unspoken prohibitions against clergy action in the secular world; instead, these religious traditions embrace modernity and maintain low boundaries between the sacred and the secular, which encourages mainline ministers and rabbis to become involved in the secular society.

One of the most central principles underlying mainline Protestantism and Judaism is the imperative to work for social justice on behalf of those whom society has left behind. In this sense the sacred has the power to transform the secular world, and the religious mission carries with it a normative prescription that the sacred exists to transform the secular by bringing the kingdom of God to Earth.[3] For Christians, this mission has been understood as the need to bring Christ's reconciliation to the world. For Jews, this mission has been defined as working diligently to repair the world. Both Christian and Jewish clergy face organizational pressure to put these missions into motion in their congregations and their communities.

We should not be surprised, then, when we hear clergywomen discussing their sacred calling to engage in activities designed to mend the secular world. When asked if their own theological beliefs encourage or discourage their involvement in politics or public affairs, 77 percent of women clergy in the national sample indicate that their theological principles either greatly encourage or encourage them to become politically engaged. Since these women would see their theological principles as core understandings of who God is and what is sacred, these results confirm the existence of a strongly shared social justice mission among mainline Protestant and Jewish clergywomen that leads them to interpret political work as a religious responsibility for the faithful.

Religiopolitical Callings

When individuals make the decision to become ordained clergy, they opt to dedicate significant portions of their lives—professional and personal —to the realm of the sacred. People who choose to enter the ministry and rabbinate often say that they do so in response to a divine calling from God.[4] Although the notion of a professional calling may also be relevant for some secular careers,[5] it takes on special importance for those in religious ministry. For clergy, when a call comes, it is as though the sacred is beckoning, and they choose to respond to it. Yet some clergy also say that they feel a sense of divine calling to be active in the secular world outside of the church or synagogue, or even via direct political action. To explore the internal dimension of religion's effect upon the political lives of clergywomen, we turn to the nature and effects of their sense of political calling.

Much of the extant literature on clergy and politics focuses on the various factors that explain differences in attitudes and participation. Religious motivations for political action are usually conceptualized in the external terms of a religious tradition's level of orthodoxy or its hierarchical organization.[6] Very few scholars have delved into the political ramifications of individual religious callings. We asked clergywomen about their political callings in an effort to understand how this internal dimension of their religious experience shapes their thinking about politics. This chapter focuses on clergywomen's interpretations of political callings and on their accounts of how these callings affect their political choices.[7]

Apart from its specific religious meaning, the term *calling* can be ambiguous, as it is sometimes used in a loose definitional sense in secular contexts. In religious settings, however, the term is understood to mean a personal message from God, especially messages about one's choice of a religious profession. A calling involves communication with God as it relates to an individual's sense of self, purpose, and relation to others in the outside world.[8] Callings come in various forms. They may be received during religious worship, daily prayer, scriptural study, or in any number of less overtly religious venues.[9] For our current purposes, we refer to a calling as a sense of being in communication with God about one's ultimate purpose in life. A clergywoman's primary calling is God's invitation to her to make the sacred realm the primary venue for her life's work. Yet she may also feel called to extend her influence beyond the sacred into the outside society.

The notion of vocation has deep roots in Protestantism; the word has its origins in the Latin Middle Ages and came into common parlance during the Protestant Reformation. The Reformation conceptualization of vocation comes from the Pauline notion of calling to salvation through Christ. The concept later came to connote labor—not just for God, but also more generally in the secular realm. The Protestant work ethic is partially derived from the Reformation conceptualization of vocation. This is not to say that God does not issue callings to people of other faiths, such as Jews, but terminology differs among religious traditions for historical and theological reasons. Nevertheless, despite the fact that one might expect mainline Protestant women to be more likely than Jewish women to mention political callings, several of the Jewish women in our study also spoke openly of their callings, using that precise term.

The vast majority of the clergywomen in the study feel that their sacred calling includes a political dimension, especially the imperative to discuss political issues. In our interviews, we are able to tease out two specific manifestations of such theological impulses. Most of the women

in our four-city study (85 percent) told us that they have personally discerned callings to speak out on political issues. Fewer women feel called
to be involved in politics outside of their congregations, but they still
account for a large proportion (73 percent) of the sample. Speaking out
on political issues seems to be much more central to a minister's or
rabbi's call to political ministry. Speaking is a specific form of preaching
and teaching, whereas political action is less closely linked to clergy's
core preaching and teaching responsibilities and requires more extensive
encounters with the secular world. Clergywomen acknowledge both
types of political callings quite frequently.

The Calling to Discuss Politics

Clergy can respond to a calling to address politics by utilizing a wide
range of cue-giving activities. Some choose to preach about issues from
the pulpit, while others address themselves to congregation members in
less public forums. They may also elect to share their views on issues
indirectly through the careful placement of bulletin inserts, posters, and
banners in the church or synagogue. Regardless of the mode of communication they choose, clergy who respond to a divine calling to discuss
political issues ordinarily say that they speak about broad political imperatives rather than narrow issues. Clergy are particularly wary of endorsing political candidates or being seen as "partisan."

   In telling us about their callings to discuss politics, clergywomen often
describe the general issue areas about which they feel most called to
speak. The women most frequently told us that they discerned a calling
to speak out for social justice—which is consistent with the longstanding
emphasis of mainline Protestantism and Judaism. Calls for social justice
might be interpreted as pleas to bring God's love to bear on the secular
realm. As a Baptist pastor explained, "I'm called to find ways to deal with
social issues." More specifically, a Lutheran minister described her calling to "talk about justice issues, hunger, racism, equality for women." A
related theme was justice—or perhaps the lack thereof—in the cities
where the women, such as this United Methodist minister, serve: "There
are times when I feel called to speak about racial injustice, class injustice
[that I see in this city]."

   Several women specifically discussed their sense of calling to address the controversial matter of homosexuality. An Episcopal priest said that she felt called to challenge her congregation to ask "why we think the way we do on issues of homosexuality . . . [and to consider] the damage that the church has done in alienating gays." The relative frequency with which the women revealed this specific calling may be related to the fact that issues tied to homosexuality (especially same-gender union ceremonies and the ordination of gays and lesbians) have been dividing mainline Protestant denominations in recent years.[10] Clergywomen, who have their own history as a controversial minority within mainline Protestantism, might be particularly sensitive to a calling to address homosexuality within their denominations. The fact that homosexuality was a common theme in this context also illustrates the low boundaries maintained by mainline Protestant and Jewish clergy between the sacred and the secular. Callings to advocate the rights of gays and lesbians would not be widespread among evangelical Protestant clergy, for example, who typically believe that homosexuality is an immoral choice rather than a natural, biological state.

Instead of discussing any particular issue area, some of the women chose to discuss their callings by explaining the importance of speaking and preaching about the gospel message of reaching out to the disadvantaged. A Baptist woman shared that her sermons often emphasize the message that Jesus Christ was not "politically correct." Christians, of course, believe that Christ himself was divine, yet he lived and worked for justice in the secular world. And as a United Methodist minister explains, "I feel called to talk to my congregation about how our community functions, and how we need to find a way to care for the folks that have fallen through the cracks." Another Methodist said she felt called to use the Bible as a source of illustrative stories for her political sermons, and she offered this example: "Here's the Samaritan woman who was an outcast, and Jesus approached her. Therefore, what are we called to do when we approach a prostitute on the street?"

Some of the women perceive a calling to educate their congregations by raising issues for debate. And denominational structures, it would seem, can facilitate action in response to such a calling, as this clergywoman relates: "One thing I appreciate about the Presbyterian Church is that when we present an issue, we need to present different sides of that issue . . . [as] an educational kind of thing." It might be reasonable to think that some clergywomen would feel uncomfortable sharing their views on issues with their congregations, but a few discern a clear calling to overcome any hesitation on that count. As a Presbyterian pastor explained, "I think it's very appropriate for them to know what my position is on an issue, and I think it's important for them to know how I arrived at that position and how it fits in with my faith, and I think it's also important that they understand very strongly that I don't expect that we're going to agree on all things." A Methodist woman echoes this approach: "I don't think that it is our responsibility to advocate one position or another, but I think it is our responsibility to encourage people to think and be open minded, to discern wisely."

Some women discuss their callings in terms of civic duty. These women do not emphasize particular issues or approaches to politics, but instead focus on the importance of applying religious principles to politics more generally. Others stress the importance of encouraging congregation members to vote or otherwise become involved in politics. An Episcopal priest typified this approach: "I always encourage people to vote. I think we are called to put our faith into action, and that is one way to do it." Similarly, said a Baptist pastor, "If an election is coming up, I'll remind people to vote." More than half—58 percent—of the clergywomen surveyed nationally also report urging the members of their congregations to register and vote. In addition, 15 percent of survey respondents organized a study group in their congregations to discuss public affairs. These sorts of activities are highly consistent with the longstanding commitment among mainline Protestants and Jews to treasure the sacred but also to lead active lives in the secular world.

These women's interpretations of their political callings as directives to educate their congregation members or to challenge their views (as opposed to converting members to a particular political worldview) are consistent with Ted Jelen's research on mainline Protestant clergy's understanding of their religious authority. According to Jelen, many mainline clergy feel that their legitimate authority is limited to encouraging their congregations to consider particular teachings. In this sense mainline clergy differ from evangelical and African American Protestant clergy. Clergy in these traditions are far more likely to embrace biblical inerrancy and thus to feel a sense of authority to tell the congregation how to behave or think, and to illustrate what is sinful, secular, or profane and what is not. Mainline clergy are unlikely to believe that they should advocate a particular political position under the rubric of biblical authority.[11]

The Calling to Take Political Action

In addition to feeling called to speak out on political matters, most of the clergywomen felt a divine imperative to engage in political action in the secular world that lies beyond the four walls of their churches or synagogues. Chapter 6 explores the many ways that these women respond to such callings through specific political activities such as protesting, campaigning, writing a letter to a newspaper editor, working with Habitat for Humanity, or serving on a government task force. The women who report feeling a calling to act emphasize three themes: involvement in the local community, direct action for social justice, and the challenge of balancing a call to political participation with other congregational responsibilities.

The most striking similarity in these urban women's interpretations of their political callings is their understanding of a calling to act locally. They were much more likely to discuss callings to act at the local level than they were to tell us about callings to change politics at the state, national, or global levels. As one Lutheran woman explained, "I feel that I must live out God's call to me where I am living here in real life." On a similar note, a Disciples of Christ pastor said, "We need to be involved in the local community around the church and realize what legislation is affecting our community." Unlike many of her colleagues, who say that their callings extend only to local action, this woman explains that she sees her calling extending beyond the local level, since local-level action "extends to the country and the world. . . . We need to be attentive to how politics affects people everywhere." Evidently most of these women are led to bridge the gap between the sacred and secular realms through local action, while others perceive callings to enter secular politics at other levels as well. Religion and politics research traditionally has focused on national-level action, which means that much of the local-level work in which these women engage has until now gone largely unnoticed.

Several clergywomen discussed the challenges inherent in living out a call to action. One theme they emphasized most heavily is the scarcity of time, one of the key pressures that affect the translation of callings into action. A Reform rabbi says, "I have to focus on the issues that are important to me, because I realize now that there are only twenty-four hours in a day." A Methodist minister explained the frustration she feels due to her attempts to juggle sacred (congregational) and secular (political) responsibilities: "I do feel strained over what I can do on a day-to-day basis. It's very difficult for me to focus on the color [of the] carpeting we are going to have in the church, and [worry about] church renovations, when there are children dying within a mile parameter of the [church] building."

Other women talked about the problem of alienating members as a result of their political action. One Presbyterian woman said she felt called to be involved in politics, but "I hope that [my congregation members] don't find out." This concern about alienating members—and in turn reducing ministerial effectiveness—came across from several women. A mixture of the principle of avoiding harm and the power of organizational pressures to avoid political controversy echoes throughout their discussions of politics, as the following chapters reveal. These concerns stem from a variety of sources. Some women worry about alienating their congregations due to the theological responsibility to reach those in need of ministry. Another important concern in many congregations is financial pressure; if a clergyperson alienates members, then those members will leave the congregation and take their financial contributions with them. Amidst these concerns for clergywomen is the added stress of attempting to maintain legitimacy in their leadership role on account of their gender, a stress that is tied to external pressures applied by the religious institutions in which these women work.

The Significance of Religiopolitical Callings

The discussions above reveal that these clergywomen's senses of political calling lead them to see politics as a legitimate aspect of their work in both the sacred and secular realms. Making political statements, and in some cases even taking political action, is integral to the missions that clergywomen see for themselves. Callings appear to have their greatest effect in the shaping of women's political priorities. For some women, the political calling directs them to specific issues, such as gay rights. Other women are drawn to general principles, such as encouraging civic engagement among members of their congregations.

Women who feel political callings work hard to educate their congregations about social justice, or at least challenge their congregations to see the connection between scripture and care for the less fortunate. In this sense they attempt, in a small way, to bridge the Durkheimian gap between the sacred and the secular. They hope to inspire others to take steps to improve the lot of those who are left behind by the callous, secular world—particularly at the local level. Yet many factors beyond political callings shape the extent to which clergywomen are willing and able to become involved in politics. All of the clergywomen in this study serve in religious traditions that strongly encourage them to engage with the secular world, regardless of their internal, personal sense of religious calling.

Religious Organizations

The fact that women clergy are *religious* professionals affects their political orientations in an internal, personal manner and also in a more external, organizational manner. Women clergy's professional lives are structured by the expectations, norms, and emphases of the religious denominations, movements, and congregations within which they work. Recall Durkheim's definition of religion: it is "a unified system of beliefs and practices relative to sacred things, . . . which *unite into one single moral community,* called a church, all those who adhere to them."[12] Religion carries with it the expectation that people who share similar beliefs will gather together for worship and fellowship, gatherings that in today's world take place within innumerable different religious traditions and congregations. It is within this external, collective manifestation of religion that clergywomen must negotiate their professional, and often political, lives. To what extent do they find the organizational structures within which they work valuable or harmful to their own political work?

Congregations and religious traditions, after all, exert sizable and varied organizational pressures on clergy with which they must come to terms.

Our study includes women serving in six mainline Protestant denominations—the American Baptist Churches, the Christian Church (Disciples of Christ), the Episcopal Church, the Evangelical Lutheran Church in America, the Presbyterian Church (U.S.A.), and the United Methodist Church—as well as rabbis serving in the Reform and Conservative movements of Judaism. After a brief discussion of the significance of religious tradition, we share the women's accounts of the political implications of their experiences within specific religious traditions.

As James Guth and his colleagues note, clergy are but one part of religious traditions with very specific histories and theological doctrines.[13] Religious traditions socialize clergy in different ways through denomination-specific seminaries, annual conferences, and official publications.[14] Such socialization is likely to lead women clergy in the same or similar religious traditions to make the same (or similar) political and social issues their priorities. In mainline Protestant and Jewish circles, heavy emphasis traditionally has been placed upon the imperative to fight for social justice wherever possible, and there is no reason to believe that seminarians do not receive this powerful socialization message.

Further, most mainline Protestant and rabbinical traditions support lobbying offices in Washington, D.C., that not only represent their faith traditions in religious policy matters on Capitol Hill but also try to provide information and other resources to clergy at the congregational level.[15] The mainline Protestant tradition embraces H. Richard Niebuhr's notion of "Christ the transformer of culture," which teaches that involvement by the faithful in the broader society is not just tolerated but encouraged and expected.[16] For example, the United Methodist Church's document on Social Principles includes the following statement: "The church should continually exert a strong ethical influence upon the state, supporting policies and programs deemed to be just and opposing policies and programs that are unjust."[17] Similarly, American Jews have long been interested and involved in politics—particularly surrounding the minority rights and civil liberties issues that are so vitally important to them.[18] These religious traditions might be expected to exert organizational pressure on women clergy (either directly or subtly) to take political action that is consistent with the traditions' predominant principles and agendas—and perhaps also to refrain from pursuing political action that is inconsistent with these principles and agendas.

To the extent that gender acts as a constraint or asset on women clergy's political choices, it does so within the structures of organized religion. Other studies have examined the challenges that women experience within the structures of organized religion.[19] But we know little about the political implications of women's gender-related experiences within these organizations. Because religious traditions vary in their historical experiences with the ordination of women, and vary also in their relative levels of acceptance of women clergy even to this day, denominational differences may emerge. In order to understand how these women see the political implications of their gender as it intersects with the religious institutions within which they work, we turn to their responses to questions about their perceptions of the usefulness of their religious traditions and their experiences as women in these environments.

The Utility of Religious Organizations

In our interviews, we asked the women whether the denominations and religious traditions in which they serve were "useful" to them in terms of political engagement. Most of the clergywomen (81 percent) mentioned that their denomination or religious tradition had somehow influenced their political priorities, action agenda, or political strategies. Their responses fall into three categories: (1) references to the religious tradition's history of social engagement; (2) mentions of a denominational group or board that organizes some political agenda; and (3) discussions of political information provided by the religious tradition's Washington, D.C., lobbying office.

More than half of all the women clergy we interviewed directly linked their interest or participation in politics to their religious tradition's historical emphasis on specific political principles. As one Presbyterian minister stated: "I have always been aware that the Presbyterian Church is actively involved in political concerns. And that has dovetailed with my family growing up, giving something back to the community. . . . So, the Presbyterian Church has clearly provided a foundation for me in terms of my political views and actions." This theme echoes in comments from women in virtually every religious tradition. As an Episcopalian rector explained, "There is a long history of concern for social issues in the Episcopal Church." A United Methodist minister said, "The United Methodist Church has always been heavily socially active; that is pretty much our whole way of coming at things." One Lutheran minister remarked that her denomination "has a commitment to those who are marginalized," and because of this commitment, she is "motivated to be helping people who are poor, alienated." Rabbis shared similar observations. As a Reform rabbi noted, "The Reform movement has been involved in social action." Another rabbi, also Reform, remarked that her movement is "very strongly committed to social justice issues and trying to follow the words of the prophets." She sees this fact as a "guiding principle for all rabbis." The women often make a clear connection between this rich history of social engagement and their own willingness to become involved in politics. In the words of a Presbyterian minister, "The theology dictates the involvement."

These women are socialized (in seminary and on the job) into their traditions' historical involvement in the fight for social justice, which subsequently influences their attitudes toward politics. The ongoing discussion of the importance of social action in these religious traditions creates a climate ripe for political mobilization. In fact, a good deal of organizational pressure to conform and to embrace the predominant set of political principles seems to exist in seminaries.[20]

A few of the Baptists and a Disciple of Christ offer a different take on the utility of their religious tradition. One Disciples minister said: "Within the denomination, we hold a very high value on individual conscience. In terms of theology, it holds a very high price on an individual's ability to interpret the Bible, and that, I think, comes through politically. The inclination, I think, of a lot of [Disciples] congregations is not to take a congregational political stance but to encourage its members to make their own." For this Disciples pastor, denominational emphasis on individual interpretation of the Bible makes her less likely to take political stands or to be engaged in the political process. Another Disciple said, "Our tradition is more [interested in] encouraging people to do what they personally feel," which resonates with her colleague's thought.

As we have seen before, all of the traditions studied here emphasize the principle that the role of a clergyperson is to help congregants think through an issue, not to tell them what to think. However, the Disciples of Christ and the American Baptists emphasize the fact that they are non-creedal religions, a fact that would give clergy even greater pause about coming across as preaching or teaching pat political stands. As one Baptist minister noted, the separation of church and state is another important principle central to Baptist heritage that may affect the political behavior of its clergy. This minister explained that the denomination "gives me a position in which I generally don't publicly express a political opinion."

Only ten of the women we interviewed failed to mention any specific ways in which their religious traditions had affected their political choices. Of these ten, four are Baptists. This apparent pattern may be another reflection of the historical emphasis upon church-state separation that is still quite strong in the American Baptist tradition (even though some Southern Baptists have shifted emphasis away from church-state separation in recent years). Of all of the religious traditions included in our study, Baptists (in this case American Baptists) are also the least hierarchical. Baptists tend to view their national organizational bodies not for the purpose of working together on social and political goals, but instead for coordinating effective mission work.[21] The fact that four of the six Baptist ministers we interviewed declined to mention their denomination as useful for their own political work reflects the relatively weak ties that exist between local congregations and larger Baptist church bodies on political matters.

In addition to giving women clergy a rich history of social engagement, denominations and religious traditions provide some women with specific opportunities for involvement. One in four women reports working in some denominational social or political organization. Denominational organizations and task forces are aimed at a wide range of social and political issues such as abortion, gay rights, world peace, and education. Denominational groups that emphasize hunger and poverty issues are one popular political outlet for many of the women clergy we interviewed. For example, two Lutheran ministers both reported serving on the same hunger task force in Milwaukee. Meanwhile, an Episcopal priest in that city said she served on a denominational group focusing on Third World development; another priest was part of a conference geared toward "figuring out how not to leave out our most marginalized citizens."

Many of the clergywomen in all four cities have served on denominational committees designed to address racism. One Episcopal priest noted that she is "one of twelve members in the denomination that are on a discernment committee on racism," a committee that is "charged to help steer the denomination to combat racism over the next umpteen number of years." Another minister, who is African American, also chaired a United Methodist Commission on Race; a third woman chaired a "cross-cultural standing committee" among Methodists in her city that addresses minority rights. She noted that she felt more comfortable working on the denominational board "as part of a group" rather than taking the lead on this issue.

Upon closer examination of which women discuss involvement in denominational advocacy organizations, the United Methodists stand out. Almost half of the women who discuss such activities are United Methodists, and most serve in Omaha (which provides some evidence of the impact of political context). Only one or two of the women from each of the other religious traditions discuss involvement in these organizations. The United Methodist Church clearly stands out for providing denominational avenues for these women to live out their calling to act politically.

Denominational organizations can also foster other types of political activity. One Lutheran minister discussed her spearheading efforts to create a "Family Life Center" in her inner-city neighborhood that would provide job training and prenatal care to the working poor. In this capacity, she worked closely with Lutheran Social Services, a regionally organized series of agencies that provide needy people with services such as alcohol and drug treatment, counseling, and older adult programming and housing.

Finally, we asked whether the women found the official Washington, D.C., lobbying headquarters supported by the various religious traditions to be helpful for their own political work. Just five women indicated that they received political support or assistance from their religious tradition's Washington lobbying office. Of those five women, four live in Washington, so access to such information might depend on proximity. This finding is not surprising in light of previous studies showing that relatively few clergy are even aware of the existence of these Washington offices.[22] As one rabbi indicated, "We are lucky to be in Washington, because we have the Union [of American Hebrew Congregations, which sponsors a lobbying office, the Religious Action Center of Reform Judaism] here. . . . As far as Jews go, the Hebrew Union is at the forefront of initiating political involvement." Lauding the center for its "well-trained, well-researched assistance," this rabbi finds that the Religious Action Center of Reform Judaism's regular bulletins about major political issues are very helpful. One Baptist minister in Washington finds the Baptist Joint Committee on Public Affairs useful for the same reason: "[They provide] us with summaries and updates on current legislation, [tell] us what it means in terms of our church and Baptists." Another minister in Washington has attended seminars sponsored by the Episcopal Church's Office of Government Relations, at which "they encourage ministers to sometimes inform their members about some legislation."

The Washington offices, while perhaps the most explicitly political organizations within these religious traditions, appear not to be very influential in the political lives of these women, especially those who do not live in the nation's capital.[23] Clergywomen are much more likely to refer to their socialization within a religious tradition or the influence of specific denominational working groups than to talk about the helpfulness of Washington offices.

Gender Experiences in Religious Organizations

Given that our interviews with clergywomen included many discussions of both the political implications of gender and the political implications of work within religious organizations, we heard surprisingly few accounts from women that link gender, denomination or religious tradition, and politics. Key exceptions to this rule are statements by several women that link concerns about issues that revolve around gender and homosexuality to personal experiences as minorities in the ministry or rabbinate. Chapter 4, which includes interview accounts of how women choose their political priorities, includes many such illustrations. In one of the few other accounts linking gender, religious institutions, and politics, a Washington rabbi noted that she is often invited to political events because she is perceived to bring unique diversity to the table as both a woman and a rabbi. Her comment was the only specific mention of gender made by any of the women in their discussions of the political utility of their religious traditions. *None* of the other clergywomen discussed their gender in response to our general question about the political utility of their religious traditions. Neither did any of the women mention denominational women's caucuses as facilitators of political action. And none discussed the growing number of women clergy in their religious traditions. Although women often mentioned gender in their answers to other questions, they did not volunteer gender-related answers in the context of how their denomination or religious tradition was useful for political action.

At least three-quarters of the women volunteered examples of how they saw their gender imposing constraints on political activity, serving as an asset for political activity, or making certain political issues more salient for them. We save accounts of the women's political priorities for the next chapter and focus here on the illustrations women provide about the implications their gender has for simply being politically active. The interview included a question about constraints on political activity. If a minister or rabbi did not mention gender in response to this question, we asked a follow-up question about whether they thought gender might pose any additional constraints. We then asked whether they had encountered any situations in which gender served as an asset for political activity.

One in every three women we interviewed indicated that gender in some way limited her ability to participate in politics, which is just slightly higher than the 28 percent of women clergy in the national study who agree with the statement that their gender makes it more difficult to become politically involved (see table 3.1). The similarity in the results between the four-city interviews and the national survey again confirms the representativeness of the experiences of the women we interviewed. The percentages of women in the two studies who see gender as a constraint on political involvement are nearly identical.

Table 3.1 Clergywomen's Views on Gender and Politics (National Survey Sample)

	Strongly Agree/ Agree	Not Sure	Strongly Disagree/ Disagree
My gender puts me at a disadvantage when it comes to upward mobility in my denomination. (*N* = 641)	55%	13%	32%
American Baptist Churches	40%	15%	45%
Disciples of Christ	62%	9%	29%
Evangelical Lutheran Church in America	62%	13%	25%
Jewish rabbis	38%	15%	47%
United Methodist Church	53%	14%	33%
My gender makes it more difficult for me to get involved in politics. (N = 636)	28%	38%	34%
American Baptist Churches	11%	49%	40%
Disciples of Christ	24%	38%	38%
Evangelical Lutheran Church in America	34%	39%	27%
Jewish rabbis	22%	44%	34%
United Methodist Church	30%	36%	34%
Because of my gender, I have easier access to opportunities to get involved in politics. (*N* = 635)	12%	41%	47%
American Baptist Churches	14%	41%	45%
Disciples of Christ	17%	39%	44%
Evangelical Lutheran Church in America	9%	38%	53%
Jewish rabbis	10%	38%	52%
United Methodist Church	12%	44%	44%

Source: Cooperative Clergy Project 2000.
Notes: Episcopalian priests were not surveyed nationally. Presbyterian ministers were not asked these specific gender-related questions in the survey. Differences between religious traditions are not significant.

Two threads of discussion in the interviews focus on gender constraints that *do not* relate closely to specific religious traditions. One Presbyterian minister argued that a woman has more trouble being accepted as a gender-neutral spokesperson: "[A] man, particularly a white man, can stand for all of humanity, but a woman can only stand for being a woman. Because of that, when I make a statement or do an action, I am conscious that there are those who might dismiss me or marginalize me because of my gender." Several other clergywomen expressed the concern that they are dismissed politically because of their collaborative leadership style, or that they amount to token women invited to political events only so people can claim that they have female representation. Another woman explained that she feels constrained because, in her opinion, people are uncomfortable around strong women.

Another source of constraint that is less closely tied to religious tradition involves the difficulty that some women clergy find in balancing family and work, or the "second-shift" problem.[24] This second-shift problem intensifies the time pressures on these clergywomen even beyond the heavy time crunch associated with the ministry and rabbinate. Some of the women we interviewed claimed that women still bear much of the burden of family responsibilities, which creates an added constraint for women clergy. One woman explained the juggling act as follows: "In one way [my spouse and child] have decreased what I do because I am aware that they need to see me. I kind of always feel that tension, what it takes to be a good mom and what it takes to be a good [clergywoman]. On the other hand, I am very aware of what kind of world that I want my son to grow up in and therefore I do feel that it is important that I speak out on certain issues." The second-shift problem can hit single mothers even harder, as another woman pointed out: "As a single parent, time is a large constraint, and the [ministry] itself is very demanding as far as hours and emotionally."

Some of the women who view gender as a constraint link it specifically to a concern about the status of women clergy within their religious traditions. They argue that women clergy are evaluated more critically than male clergy, which puts their political activity under greater scrutiny, intensifies time pressures, and leaves little time for political action. As one Presbyterian minister noted, "It is still true that women have to do a better job than men do, so women tend to spend more time with church activities and might not have as much time to participate in politics." Although the vast majority of all women clergy in the national study (99 percent) indicate that their denominations support or strongly support women in the ministry, more than half (55 percent) agree or strongly agree with the statement that their gender puts them "at a disadvantage when it comes to upward mobility" in their denominations, which indicates concern among a sizable percentage about gender issues (see table 3.1).

In our interviews, Baptist ministers were most likely to say that gender serves as a constraint on their political choices; four of the six we interviewed discussed gender as a constraint. This pattern makes sense in light of the conservatism of many variants of the Baptist faith and the longstanding gender segregation of women in that tradition. The American Baptist Churches include a stronger emphasis on biblical inerrancy than do the other Protestant religious traditions in our study. As Mark Chaves notes, adherents of biblical inerrancy tend to focus on scriptures that oppose women's ordination, so we would expect stronger opposition to women ministers within the American Baptist tradition.[25] Yet, as table 3.1 indicates, in a national sample of Jewish rabbis and clergywomen from several Protestant denominations, American Baptist women clergy were the *least* likely to agree that their gender makes it more difficult for them to become involved in politics. The differences between the experiences of the American Baptist women we interviewed and the picture presented in table 3.1 are striking. It is one of the few significant differences we see between the women we interviewed and those in our national sample. The explanation for this difference likely lies in the small number of American Baptist women in the four cities we studied. We interviewed all of the American Baptist women we could find in the four cities and came up with a total of only six, which suggests that American Baptist clergywomen are quite scarce in these cities. Thus, the American Baptist women we interviewed all work in settings in which they encounter very few other American Baptist women ministers, which may not be the case for American Baptist women who responded to the national survey. This scarcity of fellow Baptist clergywomen in the four cities may explain the fact that our interviews picked up a much higher level of vulnerability.

Previous research on congregational constraints on political action by clergy tend to assume that clergy who serve in more hierarchical religious organizations are better protected against congregational cross-pressures.[26] In terms of gender, one would expect women in the least hierarchical traditions to be most vulnerable and thus most likely to say that gender is a constraint. Yet the patterns we find in both the interview and survey data do not fit an argument that hierarchy within a religious tradition reduces gender-related political constraints. The higher level of perceived constraint among the Baptist women we interviewed is consistent with this assumption, but such is not the case for the Baptist women in the national sample. Also, in the interviews none of the Disciples of Christ women and none of the rabbis indicate that their gender is a constraint, despite the fact that these women serve in traditions with high levels of congregational autonomy. Lutherans, who serve in a more hierarchical tradition, were the second most likely to discuss gender as a constraint in the interviews. They evinced the highest level of agreement with the notion that their gender makes it difficult to become involved in politics. Consequently, our four-city study and the national sample both offer evidence that working in hierarchical religious institutions does not protect clergywomen from constraints on their political action.

One of our more intriguing findings is that nearly three-fourths of the women we interviewed were able to provide at least one example of how their gender serves as an *asset* for political involvement. One Washington-area minister discussed what she sees as women's collaborative leadership style as a political asset because it helps attract more people for political activities. Several other women noted that their gender is a political asset because it lends them credibility when they speak out on issues such as abortion or domestic violence. Some of the women feel that gender serves as an asset for political dialogue because it makes them appear nonthreatening. As one minister explained: "I can bring some issues forward and not be as threatening, because people see me as nonthreatening. So, I think I actually raise some difficult questions, and get people to think about certain issues in a comfortable way. I can use people's image that I'm soft and gentle and nonthreatening." Another woman claimed that not only do clergywomen bring a female perspective to policy discussions, but their "nurturing nature" also grants them access to the personal stories of individuals, which in turn allows them to bring to policy discussions a perspective informed by the experiences of others.

While clergywomen's minority status within their denominations and religious traditions leads some of them to see their gender as a constraint to political action, others believe that being a woman enhances their political options. Several of the women argued that they are more likely to be asked to participate in policy-related activities because a group often wants a female representative, and in some instances there are few other women clergy in the area. As one rabbi in Washington explained, the scarcity of women clergy in the community means that women clergy receive more attention, which can be a political asset.

The frequency with which the women recognized their gender as an asset cuts across nearly every religious tradition. Only Episcopal and United Methodist clergy stand out to any extent. While our interviews revealed that more than 80 percent of the women in each of the other religious traditions claim that their gender is a political asset, just one-third of the Episcopal priests agree. Interestingly, Episcopalian women in the four cities are also unlikely to say that their gender is a constraint. Perhaps the Episcopal Church's traditional emphasis on high liturgy makes the personality (and consequently the gender) of the priest somewhat less important than would be the case in somewhat "lower church" traditions, where clergy acceptance is more personality driven, or in the rabbinical scholar-leader tradition. Although the United Methodist women are also less likely than women from the other traditions to discuss their gender as an asset, more than half still describe gender as a benefit.

While most women clergy we interviewed acknowledged that gender could be an asset to their political participation, far fewer women clergy (just 12 percent) in the national sample agree or strongly agree with a statement that their gender allows them "easier access to opportunities to get involved in politics" (see table 3.1). This low percentage appears consistently among women across religious traditions. The discrepancy here stems from the different ways in which the two studies measure gender as an asset. In the interviews, we sought to get as much descriptive information as possible about how gender might be an asset, so we asked women to list any ways they could think of in which gender served as an asset. This question wording allowed us to hear a wide variety of accounts, many of which came from women who would likely disagree with the survey's general statement that gender provides "easier access." Although several of the women we interviewed did acknowledge that their gender opens doors for participation (often because political organizers seek greater diversity among participants), the appeal of gender as an asset, as we discovered during our interviews, is not limited to such opportunities. Women clergy also found that their gender lends them greater credibility on women's issues, enables them to exercise a more effective leadership style, allows them greater access to personal stories of suffering, and helps them recruit others to become involved in political and social activism. The restrictions of survey space required that the national study include only a limited number of gender questions, so the survey data measure just one of the assets that we found most interesting in the interviews: namely, access.

Conclusion

These mainline Protestant and Jewish clergywomen clearly see their theology, their religious callings, and their experiences in their own religious institutions in ways that fit our understandings of the social justice mission that they share. They embrace the political world, bridging the Durkheimian gap between the sacred and the secular. Many clergywomen feel called to become engaged in political activities that take them outside the walls of their churches and synagogues, with a special emphasis on addressing the political and social problems of the communities in which they are located. Even more women feel called to speak out on political issues, particularly those that spring from social justice and discrimination concerns.

Moreover, despite arguments concerning the weakening of denominational ties, clergywomen still clearly identify with the political connotations of their religious traditions. A majority of the clergywomen acknowledge that their denomination or tradition imbues them with empowering ideas about their role in the political world. Denominational organizations provide at least one in four of the women in the four-city study with direct access to political engagement through affiliated boards or task forces that address race, poverty, or other issues. Moreover, most clergywomen acknowledge that their denominations' rich history of social engagement has influenced their political decisions.

At the same time, their socialization within these traditions—and their experiences navigating a ministry within them as females in a male-dominated profession—shapes their political views and actions. Since the traditions covered in this study share a great deal in terms of acceptance of engagement with the secular world and emphasis on social justice, we find few stark contrasts among the different religious traditions, particularly when it comes to how women clergy view gender as an asset or constraint to their political activism.

Nonetheless, it is clear from our study that many clergywomen do believe their gender has implications for how they make political choices (not to mention for how they advance within their own denominations). The fact that many women in our interviews see their gender as an asset for political activity raises interesting questions about the political consequences of the so-called "feminization of the clergy."[27] As larger percentages of women enter the ministry and rabbinate, and as these women come to serve as mentors for successive generations of clergywomen, women clergy's orientations to and attitudes about politics are likely to change. The fact that so many women in our four-city study see their gender as an asset suggests that some of the socialization clergywomen provide for each other will include discussions about how to engage in politics in ways that acknowledge the practical advantages their gender offers.

The emphasis among these women on the advantages of their gender has an interesting parallel to an earlier study of the ways in which women clergy understand the implications of their gender for their ministry. One key finding of this study was that, when discussing how women approached ministry differently from men, clergywomen emphasized the unique *advantages* of their gender.[28] Our interviews indicate that this emphasis on the distinctively "female" contributions clergywomen make to the ministry and rabbinate remains an important aspect of the socialization and collective history of clergywomen, and that it clearly extends to clergywomen's understandings of their political roles as well. Future analysis of the national survey data will also allow us to determine whether female perceptions of gender differences outstrip actual differences in ministry style. For now, however, we remain focused on the political experiences of the clergywomen, who seek ways to live out their social justice mission within their religious institutions and through their work, which pushes them into the secular realm.

4
Clergywomen's Political Priorities

As Sidney Verba and Norman Nie observe, "the first . . . question may not be 'where does one stand on the issues?' but 'what *are* the issues?'"[1] Many people, even those who are not especially interested in politics, care deeply about certain issues to which they feel a personal connection. For instance, abortion and education are "hot-button" priorities for some individuals—such individuals are more attuned to these issues than to most others, and to the extent that they pay attention to politics, they do so in reference to the issues about which they care most. Recent research shows that having a strong interest in a particular political issue can lead one to take political action on that issue, especially when there is significant government debate surrounding it.[2] And determining "what the issues are" for clergy is made all the more important by the fact that clergy have the potential to act as opinion leaders by sermonizing on issues, encouraging congregation members to pursue outside opportunities for political participation, and even stimulating political discussion or action within their congregations.[3] In a more indirect way, through the simple acts of prioritizing and articulating their own positions on certain issues, clergy provide cues that may shape the political attitudes of their congregations. This chapter answers the question "What are the issues for women clergy?"

In light of the current political gender gap between men and women in the United States, clergywomen's political priorities may be quite distinctive. James Guth and his colleagues have shown that the vast majority of mainline Protestant clergywomen are politically liberal.[4] Some women clergy are also receptive to feminism in part because of their status as a professional minority. Even within the liberal Protestant mainline, clergywomen appear to be more sympathetic to various forms of feminism than their male colleagues. A 1983 study by Jackson Carroll and his colleagues classified 56 percent of women clergy, but only 24 percent of their male counterparts, as strong feminists; they classified only 3 percent of women clergy as antifeminist.[5] In a more recent study, more than half of the women clergy rank very high on scales of spiritual and structural feminism.[6] And this liberal and feminist orientation appears to be rooted, at least to some extent, in clergywomen's seminary experiences.[7]

In this chapter we explore the question of which political issues are most important to clergywomen. We begin by setting forth the range of issues about which women clergy say they care most. Next, we explore the extent to which the three components of our model—personal principles, organizational pressures, and external politics—appear to shape the women's issue priorities. We conclude by considering the roles that gender plays in the dynamic of setting one's own political priorities. In particular, we explore the question of whether the women care about certain issues *more* because of the experiences they have had as women.

What *Are* the Issues?

To uncover the women clergy's political priorities, we asked the women in our interviews, "What issue or set of issues concerns you most in this day and age?" We designed this question in such a way that each woman could define for herself what constitutes an issue. We were unwilling to foist a set definition of the political upon the clergywomen, and instead allowed them to determine for themselves what should count under such a rubric. The term *politics* means many things to many different people, but at root "politics is about who gets what, when, how."[8] Under this definition, the entire imaginable range of issues about which Americans debate may qualify as political, including issues that are ordinarily thought of as primarily "moral" or "social." Thus, we allow the women to impose their own understandings of what constitutes an issue of political significance in response to this question.

In our four-city study, each woman offered at least one issue that con-

Table 4.1 Clergywomen's Political Priorities (Urban Interview Sample)

Issue	*n* (Percentage)
Racism, civil rights, discrimination, intolerance	26 (48%)
Poverty, homelessness, hunger	16 (30%)
Gay rights	14 (26%)
Family and children	13 (24%)
Education	10 (19%)
Abortion	8 (15%)
Political efficacy, leaders	7 (13%)
Violence, crime, gangs, guns	7 (13%)
Women's rights, sexism	7 (13%)
Church-state issues	5 (9%)
Death penalty	5 (9%)
Foreign affairs	5 (9%)
Environment	4 (7%)
Welfare	4 (7%)
Community organizing, development	2 (4%)
Economy	2 (4%)
Health care	2 (4%)
Immigration, refugees	2 (4%)
HIV/AIDS	1 (2%)
Breast cancer	1 (2%)
Ethics	1 (2%)
Euthanasia, assisted suicide	1 (2%)
Gambling	1 (2%)

Source: Compiled by authors from interviews.
Note: Percentages represent the number of women who listed the issue area at least once among their individual set of issues of greatest concern, out of a sample of *N* = 54.

cerned her, and we count the first three issues mentioned as the issues that matter most to each woman. Table 4.1 lists the issues mentioned most frequently by the clergywomen. Nearly half of the women in our four-city study (48 percent) mentioned racism and discrimination, and nearly one-third (30 percent) listed poverty, homelessness, and hunger. Gay rights constituted the third most frequently mentioned issue, which is not surprising in light of current controversies concerning homosexuality (the ordination of gays and lesbians and the performance of same-

Table 4.2 Clergywomen's Political Priorities (National Survey Sample)

Issue	n (Percentage)
Poverty, homelessness, hunger, unemployment, socioeconomic disparity	335 (48%)
Violence, crime, gangs, guns	238 (34%)
Education	199 (29%)
Health care, HIV/AIDS	178 (26%)
Racism, civil rights, discrimination, intolerance	138 (20%)
Moral decay	132 (19%)
Environment	107 (15%)
Greed, materialism, corporate monopolies	105 (15%)
Family, children, day care	91 (13%)
Political efficacy, leaders	71 (10%)
Economy	59 (8%)
Drugs	59 (8%)
Spiritual decline	50 (7%)
Foreign affairs	33 (5%)
Elderly, Social Security	28 (4%)
Political apathy	18 (3%)
Gay rights, human rights	13 (2%)
Women's rights, sexism, abortion	10 (1%)
Ethics	10 (1%)
Church-state issues	1 (<1%)

Source: Cooperative Clergy Project 2000.
Note: Percentages represent the number of women who listed the issue area at least once among their individual issue priorities, out of a sample of N = 698.

gender union ceremonies) in some of the clergywomen's religious traditions.[9] Family and children also rank high among the women's concerns.

The national survey also asked clergy about their issue priorities, although in a somewhat different manner. Survey respondents were asked, in an open-ended question, to list up to three issues that they felt constituted the "biggest problems facing the United States today" (see table 4.2). The results presented in table 4.2 bear many similarities to those in table 4.1, but there are a few striking differences. Nationally, more women discuss poverty, including such issues as homelessness, hunger, unemployment, and the growing gap between rich and poor (48 percent), than do women in our four-city study. Women in the national sample are also more likely to list violence (34 percent) than are the women we interviewed. Also important to both sets of women are education and family issues.

In contrast, the leading issue of concern expressed among women in our interviews—racism and civil rights—was just the fifth most frequent response among women in the national sample, one in five of whom mention it as one of their most pressing political concerns. Another noticeable difference between the samples has to do with the issue of gay rights. While 26 percent of women clergy in the urban study mention this as a priority, only 2 percent of the national sample follow suit. Moreover, women in the national sample were more likely to identify violence, health care, and the "moral decay" of the nation than was the case among women we interviewed.

In general, both sets of data demonstrate that women clergy care deeply about social justice issues, particularly those that concern poverty. While the percentages vary somewhat with respect to racism, violence, and health care, all of these issues embody the social justice cause that the mainline Protestant and Jewish traditions embrace. Somewhat surprising, however, is the pointed difference on gay rights. Just 2 percent of clergywomen nationally see gay rights as among the three biggest problems facing the United States, while it registers as an important concern among a full quarter of the women we interviewed. Part of this discrepancy may be explained by the circumstances surrounding our interviews. Our interviews were conducted in 1997 and 1998, during which time the controversy over a lesbian marriage performed by Rev. Jimmy Creech in Omaha was gaining national attention.[10] This debate likely brought the issue of gay rights to the front burner among women we interviewed, especially those in Omaha. Another explanation is that urban clergy, in particular, may be more attuned to the concerns of gays and lesbians, as cities tend to have larger and more diverse populations as well as better organized gay rights advocacy groups. Most clergywomen in the national sample do not live in urban areas, so they may be less likely to confront gay and lesbian people and the special issues they face on a regular basis. Finally, the differences between the national sample and the four-city study concerning gay rights (as well as other issues) also might be due to differences in methodology, both in terms of question wording (which differed slightly between the interviews and the national survey) and format (an extensive, wide-ranging interview process as opposed to a survey question that demanded brevity). Overall, the important point is to see that women clergy in both studies share many of the same political priorities.

The Shaping of Clergywomen's Political Priorities

Our model, presented in chapter 2, includes two factors that likely play important roles in shaping women clergy's issue priorities: personal principles and organizational pressures. Certain issues have special appeal to certain people on the basis of their own personal principles and interests. Meanwhile, the organizations of which an individual is a part—either as an employee, a volunteer, or a member—often send both overt and subtle messages about which political issues matter and which should not be stressed. The political contexts within which people live and work also act to define the boundaries of discourse on political issues.

Principles

Some issues simply resonate more deeply than others for certain individuals. This feeling of attachment to particular issues flows from the myriad of factors that make each of us unique, including personal commitments, life experiences, and professional choices. Each person develops his or her own set of personal principles that guide all of life's decisions, including which political issues to prioritize.

It is our contention that a certain sort of woman is drawn to pursue a career in the ministry or rabbinate. Aspiring women clergy must feel religious callings, to be sure, but it seems that women who enter this heavily male-dominated field have additional distinctive qualities. Some of the women we interviewed seem to have decided to enter the ministry or rabbinate at least in part on feminist principle, out of a demand to be recognized as a legitimate religious voice alongside men. The mix of individuals who are drawn to the ministry and rabbinate in turn may influence the kinds of issues that matter most to them. In particular, we expect women clergy to emphasize issues often associated with feminism, such as women's rights, reproductive freedom, and discrimination more broadly construed, including racism and gay rights. Their personal interest in such issues should flow from their own principled commitment to breaking down professional barriers, as well as the history of discrimination against women in the ministry and rabbinate.

We have some evidence from our interviews that this argument carries water, as the issue about which the women most frequently expressed concern is indeed discrimination. There are many reasons to expect mainline Protestant and Jewish clergy to care about discrimination, regardless of their gender. However, the dominance of rights issues among the women's issue priorities points to a possible magnification of interest in these issues for women clergy based on their self-selection into the profession.[11] As one Disciples of Christ minister observed, "I think as an African American woman, I know firsthand what it feels like to be discriminated against, so I don't like discrimination of any sort." Moreover, if we were to combine gay rights, women's rights, and abortion with racism and discrimination to create an all-encompassing rights category, concern about rights would far outstrip any other issue area. Another take on this argument is that because mainline Protestantism and Judaism are known for their commitment to rights issues, part of the allure for women of becoming clergy might be a perception that the pulpit would offer them a forum for discussing such issues.

The question of "what is best for me?" as a member of a certain profession also contributes to the way that principles help set political priorities. Political issues that in some way affect the viability of one's status as a member of a given profession might take on increased importance. Church-state separation is the most obvious issue to which clergy (especially rabbis, as leaders of a religious minority group) might give increased attention under this rubric. Because of their minority professional status, women clergy might also feel added concern about gender equality issues. They may feel that a portion of their professional self-interest lies in the overall status of *women* clergy.

If this sort of concern about the status of one's profession is at play, then church-state relations should be a major concern among women clergy—especially Baptist ministers and Jewish rabbis, because their traditions have stressed church-state issues with special vigor. As one Conservative rabbi did observe, "Separation of church and state for us Jews, as a minority, is critical." Nevertheless, the women we interviewed are far less concerned about church-state issues than they are about other matters, especially discrimination and poverty.

Despite their relative lack of interest in this issue, there is a striking undercurrent in the women's discussions of church-state separation. Several of the women, especially rabbis, talk about this issue in the same breath that they mention the Christian Right. As one Reform rabbi said, "I can't stand the fact that [Christian conservatives] have co-opted the term 'family values.'" A sense of threat from religious conservatives also emerges from Baptist women. Other women clergy discussed their fear that conservative religious principles are being elevated to high social or legal standing, especially if this would weaken the position of women in the ministry.

Finally, the principle of preserving and protecting one's profession and professional status might motivate concern about women's rights among the clergywomen. Several said they feel a powerful sense of solidarity with the broader community of clergywomen.

Organizational Pressure

Sometimes people's interest in certain issues does not flow primarily from their personal investment in the issue, but from pressures that are exerted upon them by outside forces, such as the organizations with which are affiliated. For women clergy, organizational pressures flow from their religious denominations and traditions as well as from their congregations.

We expect women clergy to be theologically and politically liberal in part because of the socialization experiences they undergo within their religious traditions, as we have already discussed in chapter 3. The years ministers and rabbis spend in seminary have a powerful socialization effect that extends in many instances to their political attitudes and perceptions.[12] Many mainline Protestant and Reform and Conservative Jewish seminaries stress liberal approaches to scripture and politics alike. Special emphasis is placed upon the imperatives of fighting for social justice and assisting the less fortunate.[13] Indeed, these religious traditions *expect* their leaders to emphasize these issues and to address them in their congregations and sometimes even beyond.

In light of this argument, we note the importance of poverty and discrimination issues for many of the clergywomen. Tables 4.1 and 4.2 suggest evidence that organizational pressure must play some role in shaping the women's political priorities. Among the two issue areas that the women stressed most heavily were discrimination and poverty; in each case, their emphasis is highly consistent with the agendas of their religious traditions.

The women's own words also demonstrate the role that organizational pressure can play in shaping their political priorities. As a Presbyterian minister explained, "For our tradition, [social justice] is imperative. It is part of our 'blood and bone' theologically." Several women stated that their seminary experiences had played an especially important role in molding their political views. Almost all of these women told us that the seminary had a "liberalizing" effect on them. As a Lutheran pastor explained, "Seminary gave me more of an understanding of justice and a need to work towards that understanding. It taught me how to look at things from a different angle." A United Methodist woman described the effect of seminary on her political socialization in even more dramatic terms: "I grew up in a white German family, which meant that I was a Republican. Then I went to seminary, and I had to reevaluate how I looked at the world. I would say the most appropriate combination to describe my views now is Libertarian/Democrat/Socialist. Seminary was the place where I began to be a reactionary."

Beyond the socialization experiences that the women's religious traditions provide, women clergy's congregations also exert organizational pressure on them. It is rational for clergy to try to protect and enhance the congregations they serve, especially in today's competitive religious marketplace. Women clergy might find themselves drawn to social issues, such as poverty, because those issues affect people in their immediate community—or because such issues allow them to build a positive image for their churches and synagogues in order to attract and retain members.[14] Many of the women clergy we interviewed told us about programs their congregations sponsor to serve low-income individuals and children. Such programs range from food banks and clothing drives to tutoring and after-school activities. Likewise, women clergy from our national sample report that their own congregations sponsor such programs, including food pantries (80 percent), homeless shelters (40 percent), child care programs (29 percent), neighborhood kids' programs (26 percent), after-school programs (24 percent), and economic-development programs (11 percent). (See chapter 5 for a more detailed treatment of women clergy's involvement in such programs.) Given the programming and service foci of many congregations, one would expect clergy to be interested specifically in issues dealing with poverty, community development, and children and families.

Antipoverty programs, or specific emphases on children and families, may help clergywomen create distinctive community niches for their congregations. Clergy today need to keep people in the pews and money in the coffers, particularly in the face of strong competition from other religious traditions. People are drawn to churches with clear missions and messages, and local-level outreach (particularly on poverty issues) helps churches distinguish themselves.[15] It is eminently rational for clergy to make themselves as useful as possible to the people who immediately surround them. Local problems, especially poverty, create real human needs that require attention, and clergy are often among the few people in impoverished areas who have sufficient skills, resources, and willingness to address these needs.[16] Not surprisingly, many women echoed a Baptist pastor's special concern "about the gap that is widening between rich and poor."

The fact that concerns about family and children ranked so high among the women suggests a similar dynamic. Some women say that they are able to find comfortable roles for themselves in churches that might not otherwise be entirely hospitable by serving specifically as a "pastor for children's concerns." Emphasizing children's issues may also help clergy attract and keep young families, which is a primary concern in many shrinking, aging congregations.

Politics

Women clergy, like other citizens, are influenced by the public agenda, which John Kingdon defines as "the list of subjects or problems to which government officials, and people outside of government closely associated with those officials, are paying some serious attention at any given time."[17] The public agenda is shaped by a variety of political and social elites, including government officials, interest groups, and scholars. The news media play a particularly important role in shaping the public agenda. Research has shown that the American public tends to identify the issues that are stressed most heavily in network news broadcasts as the most important issues facing the nation.[18]

Dramatic events may propel an issue onto the agenda, especially if a well-organized citizen group has an interest in promoting a cause upon which the issue touches. Terrorism, for example, was thrust onto the public agenda in the wake of the 1995 Oklahoma City bombing and again on September 11, 2001. The specific nature of a given issue also has bearing upon whether it will reach the public agenda. Controversial matters such as HIV/AIDS usually take a long time to reach the public agenda, whereas issues that breed consensus, such as the need for quality education for all children, might reach it more quickly.

It is certainly possible that the drama and substance of matters that were defining the political landscape when we conducted our interviews in 1998, especially the scandal surrounding President Bill Clinton and White House intern Monica Lewinsky, might have shaped women clergy's personal priorities just as they transformed the public agenda. If so, then we will observe the effect of external politics—one of the components of the model we set forth in chapter 2—on the political priorities of women clergy. Media attention to the Clinton-Lewinsky scandal put presidential impeachment and the sexual behavior of elected officials on the public agenda during the time period when we interviewed the clergywomen.

The Gallup Organization tracks the American public's views on the question "What do you think is the most important problem facing this country today?" In 1998, the year in which the Clinton-Lewinsky matter was the chief news story, crime and drugs ranked highest in the Gallup poll, with economic problems and the deficit comprising a second tier.[19] As table 4.1 shows, some of the issues that women clergy prioritize do reflect the public agenda as measured by Gallup, but by no means do the women's political priorities appear to be a mirror image of the public agenda. Only seven of the women we interviewed mentioned violence and crime, and only two women said that economic issues were among their greatest concerns, even though these issues topped the Gallup poll.[20] Meanwhile, seven women listed issues related to political efficacy and political leaders. A United Methodist pastor expressed her concern about "the viability of our current form of government. I don't think the system as it currently works can continue. . . . Even the most honest person elected today . . . would have to compromise so much that [their] integrity would be lost. . . . The system has become an entity unto itself. . . . It's going to take a lot for it to change." Concerns about political efficacy and political leadership might have been magnified by the media's nearly exclusive emphasis on the Clinton-Lewinsky matter. We heard almost no specific comments about this scandal from the women clergy, however.

The distinctiveness of the women's political priorities vis-à-vis the public agenda shows that women clergy focus most upon their own broader moral concerns regarding the ordering of politics instead of simply following trends set by the general public. Nevertheless, the public agenda should not be written off as an unimportant predictor of clergywomen's issue interests. It is certainly possible that the women's prioritization of gay rights demonstrates a public agenda effect, considering that the battles over homosexuality were among the most salient issues *within organized religion* during 1998. As one Presbyterian woman observed, "Inside the church, the big issue right now concerns homosexuals, especially their ordination." The answer to the question of "what the issues are" is evidently more keenly subject to other factors, such as the salience of gender in the women's professional and political lives. It is useful to acknowledge, however, that the vicissitudes of the public agenda and current political events may help to shape clergywomen's political priorities.

Gender's Effect on Clergywomen's Political Priorities

Given that the construct of gender carries myriad ramifications, the very fact that the clergy under study here are all *women* must play a role in shaping their political priorities. It is an inescapable fact that women clergy constitute only a small minority within their profession. Many scholarly accounts of women clergy's career paths report that they face significant personal and professional constraints.[21] Perhaps the clergywomen we interviewed feel a special attraction to certain political issues because they are women; gender itself may carry a special salience for them.

In our four-city study, we asked the clergywomen whether they felt an increased affinity for any political issues because of their gender. Fully 57 percent (thirty-one women) said that they did care about certain issues more passionately because they are women. Only sixteen women (30 percent) said their issue concerns were not tied in any way to their gender, and seven others (13 percent) were unsure. On the whole, three themes emerge from the clergywomen's explanations of how gender shapes their political priorities: (1) the effect of the *general* experience of being a woman; (2) the effect of being a woman *in the clergy profession;* and (3) the absence of any gender effect. Responses that fit into the first category address the effects of women's own experiences upon their issue concerns: for example, "I care about education because I am a mom" or "Women have difficulty getting respect because of their collaborative leadership style." We might expect to hear similar comments from women regardless of their profession. Responses in the second category, however, are specific to the experience of working in a male-dominated profession, such as "I care about discrimination because I have experienced it on the job" or "Because there are so few women clergy, I get invited to participate in more activities."

Gender's General Effects

Listening to women's explanations of how being female has led them to prioritize certain political issues offers an opportunity to search for effects of gender-based socialization. Women clergy's socialization process begins in childhood, when they are socialized into gender roles, and continues with adult socialization into family roles.[22] Clergywomen are further socialized in seminary and later in congregational settings. Undoubtedly this socialization process has important implications for their perceptions of what it means to be a woman, what it means to be a woman minister or rabbi, and how these self-perceptions influence their reactions to political issues. We focus primarily on how clergywomen's experiences *as women* are germane to the nature of the issues that they say are most important to them. Our analysis therefore examines the end result of socialization more than the socialization process itself.

Recall that thirty-one women told us that their gender plays a role in their prioritization of issues. For these women, certain political issues seem to carry added salience because of their life experiences as women. A United Methodist woman said she simply reacts to issues "differently, more affectively. . . . It's the feeling of the experience; it's not [just] thinking about it. . . . Women are encouraged to feel things more." The women also express keen concern about gender roles in today's society. As a Disciples of Christ pastor said, "I worry about the rise of patriarchy. I see megachurches going up, and you can watch the folks go in with papa and mama and string of children . . . white, upwardly mobile. . . . Is this what is becoming mainstream? What will happen to our sisters?" A Presbyterian woman added, "Living as a woman in this day and age, I can't help but be aware of the issues that seem to affect women across the board. Issues of poverty, issues of safety, issues of just basic concern for reproductive choice . . . absolutely gender plays a role." One's gender-related family ties also matter, as a rabbi noted: "As a mom, I am especially concerned about school and education issues."

Other women tied gender to health concerns about women's bodies. A United Methodist pastor observed, "I've noticed that women in particular would be concerned about healing issues." Several women said that reproductive choice ranks high among their priorities because of their gender but acknowledged the loaded nature of that issue. A Lutheran pastor expressed this frustration: "When you talk about reproductive rights, you're talking about an issue where the so-called anti-choice folk[s] refuse to believe that women have the competence to make those decisions for themselves." Another health issue, breast cancer, concerned one rabbi because of both her gender and her heritage: "[Breast cancer] affects women, but also . . . some *Jewish* women are most susceptible to getting breast cancer."

Some of the women tied their prioritization of children's issues and poverty to their gender. A Baptist minister stated, "Part of my interest in children's issues is because I never had children myself, so there was this attraction to it." An Episcopal priest made a similar comment. As a Disciples of Christ pastor explained, "[Being a woman] gives me sensitivity and insight that male clergy do not have. . . . Jesus always seemed to be holding out for the person on the fringe. A lot of white men have no clue what that really is about." A United Methodist minister told us that she cares more about poverty issues as a woman "because I have seen so many women put in circumstances [where] they have to suffer. There is still inequity in pay, as well as advancement in jobs." The general sentiment of another Methodist woman was quite straightforward: "If you are a woman you always have to be on the side of the oppressed." A Lutheran woman spoke along similar lines: "When you talk about welfare reform, you are talking about women, primarily, and children."

The Effect of Being a Clergywoman

Women's experiences in the clergy profession seem to lead them to prioritize discrimination issues. Many women told us that their experiences with gender-based discrimination in the ministry and rabbinate have led them to pay more attention to rights issues and the need for greater inclusiveness. In particular, the women's experiences with prejudice and exclusion have created a deeper concern within them about the politics of discrimination. As a Presbyterian woman explained, "I think the racism issue and . . . [homosexuality] affect me more because I am part of a gender that for a long time was excluded and is particularly excluded from the ordained leadership in the church."

Several women argued that their standing in the profession has inspired them to challenge the status quo, particularly concerning issues of equality. According to a Presbyterian, "Women have a special responsibility to articulate their politics in particular ways because we stand on the shoulders [of those] who stood before us. When it comes to issues of equality, then perhaps women clergy do have a particular need to get involved." Another Presbyterian explained that she was breaking gender barriers in her denomination and claimed that "because of who I am, I am reminded that I cannot be just part of the status quo." Moreover, a United Methodist woman noted that "as a woman, I have been aware of gender issues in a way that I had not ever realized, and because of the things that I have experienced at times. I hope that has made me more sensitive to how other people are treated, including by me, because of the nature of the structures that we live in." An additional Methodist discussed her frustration with the prejudice that she has faced and argued that it has opened her eyes to ongoing problems with discrimination:

"When I discovered that . . . the United Methodist Church has been ordaining women since 1956, I expected that the church would be relatively friendly to women, but my first [congregational position] was very much troubled by issues of them not wanting a woman pastor."

Women who tell stories of personal experiences with professional gender discrimination are more likely to say they prioritize certain issues more than others because they are women.[23] However, these women are only slightly more likely to include discrimination among their political priorities. Women clergy who do not relate personal stories of professional discrimination list other reasons why they would also care about discrimination. Their reasons include their religious traditions' emphasis on social justice and their general understanding of the "challenged" position of women in the ministry and rabbinate. The extent to which these women articulate a shared notion of this challenged position is evident in the fact that nearly all of them eloquently discuss the professional challenges that face women clergy *in general,* even though most add that they *personally* had not faced such challenges. In fact, only three clergywomen in our interviews told stories of personal experiences with discrimination.

Although women serving in a variety of denominations told us about specific challenges that women face due to discrimination in their profession, United Methodists stood out because they explained how this challenge—and their gender—specifically affects their embrace of gay rights as an issue. The United Methodist women may have been more sensitive to issues of discrimination at the time of the interviews because they occurred in the midst of the Jimmy Creech controversy in Omaha. (Incidentally, Creech was subsequently stripped of his ministerial credentials by a United Methodist tribunal.) This context might have made the issue of discrimination—and on another plane, the vulnerability of a minister's position—even more relevant for United Methodist women. Methodist clergywomen may also experience additional challenges because of the enormous political diversity of their denomination. There are quite a few more conservative ministers within the United Methodist Church who might challenge women than would be the case in other mainline Protestant traditions.[24]

Is Gender Irrelevant?

A few women who emphasized the need to fight discrimination nevertheless explained that this issue did *not* concern them more because of their gender. Two such women argued that they did not think gender played a role in their prioritization of discrimination because their husbands shared their political concerns. As one Presbyterian woman noted, "My husband is much more liberal than I am, and when I am tempted to take a more moderate view, he pushes me to be more liberal. He is very big on women's equality issues." One of these women later backed off a bit to say that her experience as a mother may have affected her views. "I think my husband would answer the same thing and would have the same sorts of concerns. So no. [Gender does] not necessarily [matter. But] maybe being a mother has affected my views." An Episcopal priest's family background had a bigger effect on her political views and actions than have her experiences as a woman or as a minister: "It was my upbringing more . . . I grew up in a political family." Another Episcopal priest notes, "In my congregation I am not identified as the woman here for women." And a Baptist pastor expresses a different kind of concern: "I don't want [issues] to concern *men* less because of their gender."

The Significance of Gender-Based Experiences

Over half of the clergywomen argue that their gender shapes their answers to our query about which issues concern them most. Some issues are more salient for women either because they relate specifically to the female body or because they resonate more fully with the experiences of women than with those of men. The women's responses square with the argument that the social processes that influence which women enter the ministry and rabbinate—as well as the socialization experiences they subsequently undergo in the profession—combine to result in higher levels of support for liberal causes. Note especially that those who emphasize women clergy's status differential focus their political priorities on discrimination and the need to change the structures that perpetuate it.

Women clergy's overwhelming support for reducing discrimination is undoubtedly also bolstered by the political norms their religious traditions emphasize, via subtle socialization and more overt organizational pressure. In mainline Protestantism and Judaism, socialization in seminary and in the profession creates a strong awareness of social justice concerns, including discrimination. Many male clergy who serve in these traditions also express concern about such issues, as do other women in our sample who do not make gender arguments.[25] However, the women whose views are portrayed here not only see discrimination issues as important, they perceive their concern about these issues to be tied fundamentally to the gender-based experiences they have had within their own religious traditions.

Conclusion

It is quite clear that women clergy's political priorities diverge sharply from the issues that top the public agenda. Unlike many citizens in other walks of life, clergywomen prioritize issues on the basis of considerations that go far beyond what they see, hear, and read in the news media. Due to a plethora of mutually reinforcing influences, from their personal experiences as women to their status as an underappreciated professional minority to the strong socialization effect of learning about and working within mainline Protestantism and Judaism to their desire to protect their professional status, women clergy are exceptionally committed to social justice issues, especially discrimination and poverty. They also pay persistent attention to the core social justice issues of poverty and public order.[26] And previous research shows that these issues remain as women clergy's top political priorities from one decade to the next, which conveys a sense of permanence about their general orientation to politics.[27]

The issues that stimulate less passion in the women may be more likely to shift as the public agenda shifts. For example, it may be that the women did not rank foreign policy issues among their top priorities because there were few international crises in 1998 or in 2000. It stands to reason that the women's levels of interest and concern about issues that are not among their greatest, most longstanding priorities may be more likely to wax and wane with the public agenda. It is in this secondary way that external politics affect clergywomen's political priorities.

Both commitment to social justice and feminist socialization provide a rationale for many women clergy to engage in political action. Likewise, their socialization experience as a professional minority gives them a unique vantage point from which to view issues of discrimination. The passion and conviction with which these women view such issues make clergywomen a valuable resource for political groups that champion progressive causes.

As more women enter the ministry, the commitment of women clergy to liberal and feminist agendas might continue to grow, and women may come to feel more empowered and committed to action on issues of discrimination upon meeting female colleagues with similar views. They may also become increasingly frustrated by the "stained glass ceiling": the notion that, despite the increasing numbers of women in the ministry, women are still appointed to relatively low-prestige positions and find it difficult to advance professionally. If this networking factor proves highly salient, then we would expect women clergy's priorities to continue to shift toward more liberal emphases as more women clergy join the ministry.[28]

The case of discrimination is particularly instructive. The women's prioritization of discrimination highlights the role gender plays in the translation of personal and professional experiences into political attitudes. The emphasis that these women place on issues of discrimination also appears to support speculation that the influx of women into the ministry will exacerbate tensions between liberal and conservative religious camps by moving the liberal camp further to the left.[29] However, jumping immediately to this conclusion ignores the ways in which women clergy's experiences may change as more women enter the ministry. As women clergy become more numerous and widely accepted, feminist paradigms may become less relevant and therefore less likely to shape women clergy's political attitudes.[30]

Women clergy have the potential, especially once their numbers grow even further, to set a broad political agenda for their congregations and possibly to influence the broader agendas of their religious traditions. Their personal political priorities are of great importance for this reason, but one day women clergy may also have the power to shape the *public* agenda. Herbert Blumer argues that issues have life courses that span from the moment of society's initial recognition of the existence of a problem through the resolution of the problem.[31] Recent research suggests that "early recognizers" of social problems may be influential in placing issues on the public agenda in the first place.[32] Because women clergy are uniquely situated as female (and in many instances feminist) voices in a social institution that is designed explicitly to provide moral guidance, they may have the potential to act as agenda setters not only for their congregations or denominations but for American society more generally. We now move to a consideration of whether clergywomen choose to *take political action* to address the issues about which they care most.

5
Clergywomen's Political Action Agendas

Sometimes people who complain about political issues are criticized for failing to take political action to change the things about which they complain. Nevertheless, scholars have demonstrated that personal concern about specific political issues often does mobilize people to address such issues using political means.[1] The link between political interest and action, however, is neither uniform nor entirely predictable. Many citizens eschew activism, even when it comes to the issues that they care about most passionately. On the other hand, some citizens find themselves involved in political work regarding issues about which they actually have little personal concern. What factors combine to shape the substantive content of clergywomen's political activity, which we call their *action agendas?*

Political scientists focus on issues when they study public opinion, but rarely do they emphasize issues in studies of political participation. In one of the few studies that take citizens' issue priorities seriously, Steven Rosenstone and John Mark Hansen demonstrate that personal concern about specific political issues can motivate people to take action to address those issues.[2] There has been very little analysis, however, of whether people actually take political action to address the specific issues that most concern them—or of the factors that heighten this consistency for some people and make it more difficult for others. Our interview data, however, allow this kind of mobilization analysis for clergywomen. In the last chapter we saw that the women express great concern about social justice issues, especially those that relate to economic disparity and discrimination. Using women's own accounts from the interviews, in this chapter we present a detailed assessment of the extent to which they actually take political action to address these two issue priorities. We then compare the experiences of women whose priorities and action agendas match to the experiences of those who do not display such consistency. Specifically, we use our interview data to see how principles, organizational pressures, and politics mobilize some women to take action on their top priorities—but lead other women to refrain from acting on their priorities, and instead perhaps to take action on issues that are not priorities for them.

As we note in chapter 2, our work here builds on theories that stress issue mobilization, organizational mobilization, and recruitment. Women whose priorities and actions match up show us how such priority-action consistency stems from their own personal passion for these issues, which complements issue mobilization theory. However, consistency between a clergywoman's own personal political priorities and the substantive content of her political action does not necessarily mean that she is mobilized primarily by her own passion for an issue. Organizational pressure and recruitment play roles as well. This is especially true for clergywomen, as their priorities often are rooted in a strong set of religio-political principles, reinforced by organizational pressure.

Our interview data provide insight into the complex interactions of these mobilization dynamics. At the same time, our national survey data allow us to see whether similar patterns emerge among clergywomen across the country. Before turning to interview accounts that help us understand why clergywomen take political action on some issues and not on others, we explore the baseline question of how often and in what capacity women clergy engage in political action to address the issues that they prioritize most highly.

The Content of Clergywomen's Action Agendas

We refer to the substantive nature of women clergy's political activities as their action agendas. Chapter 6 offers a more comprehensive analysis of their political *strategies:* the actual political tasks that they undertake both in and out of their churches and synagogues. In this chapter, how-

Table 5.1 Clergywomen's Action Agendas (Urban Interview Sample)

Issue	Action Agenda Involvement n (Percentage)
Poverty, hunger, homelessness	35 (65%)
Community organizing, development	13 (24%)
Education, family, and children	13 (24%)
Racism, racial tension, discrimination, intolerance	12 (22%)
Abortion	10 (19%)
Gay rights	9 (17%)
Immigration, refugees	5 (9%)
Women's rights, advancement	5 (9%)
Death penalty	3 (6%)
Violence, guns, gangs	3 (6%)

Source: Compiled by authors from interviews.
Note: N = 54 respondents.

ever, we focus on the *substantive* nature of their activity: about which issues do they choose to take action?

In our interviews we asked women, "What specific social or political projects have you been involved with lately?" We code the activities that they mentioned according to their substantive issue focus. If, for example, a woman indicated that she was involved with her church's soup kitchen or its local Habitat for Humanity chapter (or both), we code her as being involved in the "poverty, hunger, and homelessness" category. Table 5.1 shows the four-city women's involvement in political activities apropos of ten different issue areas.

Women were most likely to say that they engage in actions designed to address poverty, hunger, and homelessness. Second most common are education issues and those dealing with community organizing or development. These findings are not surprising given the strong social justice background of the women's religious traditions. Yet women clergy also frequently report working in more controversial areas as well addressing such issues as abortion and gay rights.

The national survey also allows us to assess clergywomen's action

Table 5.2 Clergywomen's Action Agendas (National Survey Sample)

Issue	Percentage Spending Personal Time
Poverty, Homelessness, Hunger	
Food pantries	46%
Homeless shelters	30%
Home repair or home building	18%
Education, Family, Children Child care	17%
After-school programs	18%
Programs for neighborhood kids	20%
Education programs	24%
Homosexuality, HIV/AIDS	
Ministry to gays and lesbians	30%
HIV/AIDS support	16%
Other	
Race-relations programs	26%
Economic-development programs	11%
Police, gang, or crime programs	11%
International programs (famine relief, human rights)	26%

Source: Cooperative Clergy Project 2000.
Note: N = 698 respondents.

agendas, as displayed in table 5.2. Notice that the women in this sample report spending time working on issues similar to those emphasized by the urban women (compare tables 5.1 and 5.2). An important caveat is in order, however. The survey instrument asked clergy whether they had taken action on a finite set of issues only; there were no free-response items about action. Thus it is quite possible that the clergy in the national sample undertake actions to deal with issues that were not included in the survey battery. (Indeed, one of the benefits of our four-city study is that clergy had the opportunity to explain *all* of their political activities in great detail.) We might therefore view the national data as a likely low estimate of the real content of clergywomen's action agendas.

Nonetheless, the national survey data largely mirror the results from our four-city study. The "poverty, homelessness, hunger" category again leads the way; almost half of women clergy nationally report spending personal time working with food pantries in particular (46 percent). Whereas one-quarter of the urban women report working on issues surrounding education, family, and children, the figures range from 17 to 24 percent nationally. Comparable percentages of both samples also report working with race-relations programs. One difference that does emerge is that the women in the urban sample report spending more time on community organizing and development (24 percent) than do clergywomen nationally (11 percent). This difference is likely a reflection of the urban context; community-development programs are undoubtedly more prevalent in cities than in suburbs and rural areas.

What sorts of consistencies and discrepancies exist between the clergywomen's issue priorities and their action agendas? Table 5.3 compares clergywomen's issue priorities and action agendas in five broad substantive categories: poverty, hunger, homelessness; education, family, children; racism and discrimination; community development; and crime and violence. Both samples were asked questions about these five categories. We also include three priority-action comparisons that carry specific gender or discrimination dimensions (abortion, women's rights, and gay rights) for which we have data from the four-city sample only.

Figures in the table that are underlined are cases in which clergywomen take more action on an issue than their personal list of priorities would suggest. The table demonstrates that clergywomen—both in our urban study and nationally—are much more likely to *take action* on poverty, hunger, and homelessness than they are to profess that such matters rank among their top issue *priorities*. A similar pattern emerges for both sets of women regarding economic development and community organizing. For the women in the four-city study, the other six issues listed elicit the opposite effect. These women were more likely to say that education and family-related issues, race relations, crime, women's rights, and gay rights rank among their issue priorities than they are to take action on them. Nationally, however, the picture is somewhat different. Women clergy in the national sample are slightly *more* likely to take political action on education, racism, and family- and child-related issues than they are to list such issues among their top personal priorities.

Table 5.3 Priority–Action Agenda Comparison

Issue	Urban Sample		National Sample	
	Priority (Percentage)	Action (Percentage)	Priority (Percentage)	Action (Percentage)
Poverty, hunger, homelessness	*30*	*65*	*48*	*58*
Education, family, children	43	24	29	41
Racism, racial tension, discrimination, intolerance	48	22	20	26
Community organizing, *economic development*	*6*	*24*	*5*	*11*
Crime, violence, guns, gangs	13	6	34	11
Abortion	*15*	*19*	—	—
Women's rights, advancement	13	9	—	—
Gay rights	26	17	—	—

Sources: Compiled by authors from interviews; Cooperative Clergy Project 2000.
Note: Italicized figures represent cases in which level of action outstrips level of prioritization. Categories offered in the national survey do not precisely match categories offered in the urban study.

Clearly there are no easy conclusions to draw in answering the question of whether and why clergywomen choose to take action on the issues that they prioritize most highly. To bring more focus to this inquiry, we now spotlight priority-action consistency surrounding two issue concerns that lie at the heart of the social justice mission embraced by so many of these women clergy: economic disparity and discrimination. These two matters were, as chapter 4 shows, two of the most common areas of concern among the clergywomen.[3] Do their action agendas correlate with their prioritization of these two key issues? In the analysis that follows, we rely exclusively on the insights gathered from the women we interviewed. The interview context allowed these women to offer detailed explanations of why they choose specific issues to tackle politically.

Priority-Action Consistency on Economic Justice and Discrimination

The religious organizations within which women clergy most frequently work typically champion social justice issues such as economic disparity and discrimination.[4] In many mainline Protestant denominations, such concern is highly consistent with a deeply rooted principle that religious people should be actively involved in the culture, addressing the problems of the less fortunate in a "Christlike" manner.[5] Within Jewish circles there are similar concerns about social justice issues that stem from the intense battles for justice Jews have fought for millennia and from overt teachings about the normative appropriateness of pursuing activism for the sake of justice. The idea that prevailing norms about the need for God's people to work for justice lead clergywomen to act on their priorities indicates that issue mobilization is for them reinforced by principles. Because clergy's work involves them intimately in the preaching and teaching of such principles, it should not be surprising to find them striving personally to live up to their religiopolitical principles.

Economic justice issues, broadly defined, are the religiopolitical bread and butter of mainline Protestant and Jewish congregations and denominations.[6] It is very common to find mainline churches and synagogues sponsoring soup kitchens, clothing banks, and programs to fight homelessness. In fact, it is rare to find a mainline congregation that does not report at least some level of involvement in activities designed to ame-liorate poverty. We therefore expect women clergy to have little difficulty translating their concern about economic justice into action. The wide-spread presence of antipoverty programs within the women's religious organizations means that the women are often expected to take leader-ship roles in such programs, or at least to fit participation in them into their already time-stretched schedule. On the other hand, the fact that antipoverty programs are usually well established in churches and syna-gogues makes such programs a convenient venue for clergywomen's po-litical participation. And it is unlikely that any clergy who get involved in antipoverty programs face or perceive significant resistance from their congregations as a result. Thus organizational pressures play an impor-tant role in shaping the women's action agendas, often working in con-cert with issue mobilization.

Discrimination has long been a special concern of mainline Protes-tants and Jews, both of whom were visibly supportive of the civil rights movement.[7] Civil rights activism established organizational traditions of fighting discrimination within both mainline Protestantism and Juda-ism. Issues related to discrimination might also hold special resonance for women clergy because they serve in a male-dominated profession in which their very legitimacy is often called into question. These personal experiences may strengthen their commitment to the principle of fight-ing discrimination in all its forms.

Unlike economic justice, discrimination can and does engender con-troversy in mainline Protestant and Jewish circles. There is much less agreement about how to address matters of women's equality, racism, and especially homosexuality than there is about the imperative to fight pov-erty. As such, we would expect that it is quite a bit riskier for women clergy to translate their concern about discrimination into concrete, pub-lic action, since doing so might polarize their congregations and jeopar-dize their source of livelihood. Such circumstances point to the ways in which mobilization forces can counteract one another. Issue mobiliza-tion may be overwhelmed by organizational pressures, which would pre-vent women who prioritize discrimination from acting on those con-cerns.

Politics might also prevent action on discrimination-related issues. In

Table 5.4 Priority-Action Consistency and Inconsistency (Urban Interview Sample)

	Economic Justic n (Percentage)	Discrimination n (Percentage)
Consistent		
Not interested, does not act	9 (17%)	10 (19%)
Interested and acts	29 (54%)	30 (56%)
Inconsistent		
Interested, does not act	6 (11%)	8 (15%)
Not interested, acts	10 (19%)	6 (11%)

Source: Compiled by authors from interviews.
Note: N = 54 respondents.

one instance, clergywomen may be recruited for other political projects and thus be left with insufficient time to work on discrimination issues. In another instance, a pressing problem, such as a spike in homelessness, might lead some women to refocus their attention even if their personal priorities lie in other issue areas. Thus both organizational pressures and politics can lead women to act on issues that are not among their top priorities.

Priority-action consistency and inconsistency may each manifest itself in two forms. Some women display consistency by indicating neither interest in nor activity on either economic justice or discrimination. Others are consistent in a different way because they display both interest in and activity on one or both issues. Likewise, inconsistency takes two forms. Some women express little interest in an issue but nevertheless take action to address it, whereas other women are keenly concerned about an issue on which they do not act. Table 5.4 reports the frequencies of priority-action consistency and inconsistency for the two issue areas of economic justice and discrimination. As the table shows, the majority of the women clergy show consistency in their levels of interest and action on both economic justice and discrimination. The rest display a mismatch, or inconsistency.

In chapter 2, we identify three factors—principles, organizational pressure, and politics—that work to shape clergywomen's political priorities and the nature of their political actions. Chapter 4 explores how these three factors affect the women's political priorities. Here we turn to analysis of these factors to sort out the reasons why consistencies and inconsistencies appear between the priorities and action agendas of these clergywomen. We see in chapter 4 that the women's political priorities are often grounded in social justice principles. Do these same principles help push women to act on social justice concerns? Are there other competing principles that work to discourage action on political priorities, particularly controversial ones? Personal concern about an issue might motivate action to address that issue in a direct, uncomplicated fashion. Organizational pressure should also play a role; a group to which one is tied might offer strong encouragement—or discouragement—when the time comes for a clergywoman to decide whether to take political action surrounding a particular issue. And because simply being asked is often a significant reason for a person to become involved in political action, we add recruitment as an explanation under the third factor, politics, now that our attention is shifting to the concrete political actions that the women take. Taken together, these three factors help us to understand why women clergy may elect to take political action—or abstain from doing so—to address economic justice and discrimination.

Priority-Action Consistency

Some women lack both interest in and action on either economic justice or discrimination, as the first row of table 5.4 displays. For some, the choice not to engage in action on economic justice or discrimination is a matter of not expending political energy on issues that do not rank among their top political priorities. Other women simply emphasize their apolitical nature. In the words of one Disciples of Christ pastor, political involvement does "not come naturally." A rabbi told us that she simply does "not feel politically astute." Gender also plays a role in discouraging some women from acting on their top priorities, as a Presbyterian minister explained: "People's expectations of clergywomen, in many ways, [create constraints]. We are encouraged to be polite, and political activity is not necessarily seen as polite."

Another factor that emerges among these politically disengaged women is the demobilizing organizational pressure of time constraint. After all, for busy clergywomen, political activity cannot take precedence over ministerial duties.[8] For example, one of the Lutheran ministers is a single parent who admits that "time is a large constraint, and the job is very demanding as far as hours, and emotionally." A Presbyterian minister further linked her time constraints to her gender: "It is still true that women have to do a better job than men do, so women tend to spend more time with church activities and might not have as much time to participate in politics."

Other clergywomen, however, display priority-action consistency in that they express concern about and take action to address economic justice or discrimination. This stance is reflected by the second row in table 5.4. Political passion for an issue can directly mobilize an individual to take political action pursuant to that issue.[9] The person's own concern about—or feeling of connection to—the issue mobilizes her participation. This sort of priority-action consistency is often a sign of what Rosenstone and Hansen call "issue mobilization."[10] When clergywomen act on their political priorities out of personal passion, issue mobilization has occurred. For example, a clergywoman told us that she is something of a pro-choice activist because "I am definitely concerned about the abortion issue, which I see as a right of women to handle their own bodies." We would expect this sort of issue mobilization to play a role in the political lives of clergy, especially because they encounter many opportunities to speak publicly about issues that matter most to them.

We frequently found women clergy acting directly upon the economic justice or discrimination-related concerns that they personally prioritize. For these women, prioritization of the issues themselves appears to mobilize their activity. Our narratives repeatedly reveal women clergy who are passionate about poverty, hunger, gay rights, and women's issues who then decide to express this passion in political ways. For example, a Baptist minister notes that she feels "strongly about the poor." She believes "it is important to be involved in people's lives" when they have less than she does. Alternatively, a Presbyterian minister links her activism surrounding gender discrimination to her personal experience: "Having experienced discrimination, I think the issue isn't abstract. It is personal in my life. But that gives me a real sense of what other women go through, live with, and I think it also has given me more of an identity with other rights issues, around race, around sexual orientation."

The women who display this form of priority-action consistency explain that their concern about an issue mobilizes them directly for action. A Baptist minister reflects a common concern regarding economic justice: "I worry about people who are locked in a cycle of poverty and can't get out." This same minister helps with her church's food pantry and has marched in support of antipoverty causes, particularly those involving children. Regarding discrimination, a United Methodist minister expresses her profound political concern for "multicultural understandings, breaking down the barriers of racism," and gay rights. These concerns have led her to participate in AIDS walks and to tackle a variety of civil rights concerns.

Priority-Action Inconsistency

Many clergywomen do not display great consistency between their issue priorities and their action agendas. The group reflected in the third row of table 5.4 fail to take action on the issues about which they care most. It is often a challenge for women clergy to act on the issues they personally prioritize in the face of congregations that are not supportive of their political activities, particularly if the activities are related to controversial matters such as abortion or homosexuality. In these instances demobilization from organizational pressures competes against issue mobilization. For example, a Presbyterian minister remarks that her congregation is somewhat discouraging and hypersensitive when it comes to HIV/AIDS. While she did undertake political work with a statewide AIDS project, she tried not to let people know and described her participation as "incognito." A United Methodist woman notes that her congregation is very conservative, so she refrains from mentioning homosexuality or abortion: "I do some stuff personally, but I don't pull the church in."

On the other hand, some of the clergywomen display a different sort of priority-action inconsistency by taking action on issues that do not rank among their top priorities. As the fourth row of table 5.4 shows, there is moderate evidence of this phenomenon, especially around economic justice: ten women were devoting time to addressing this issue area despite the fact that they had higher personal priorities. Most often these women were undertaking economic justice work through established political and social work programs in their own congregations. Doing so was an attractive option for them in some cases because they lacked sufficient time to pursue other political avenues and in other cases because economic justice is a relatively noncontroversial area for political activism.

We were surprised to hear relatively few women saying that they fear taking action on the issues that concern them most. As table 5.4 shows, we more often found women being proactive politically—even on issues that do not rank among their top personal priorities. For discrimination, action without interest is less common than interest without action. Despite the reasonable expectation that women clergy would face more substantial constraints against taking action on controversial discrimination issues than would be the case for economic justice, there is no real difference in priority-action consistency between the two issues. What factors might be encouraging these women to be involved politically, despite the risks such activity might bring?

Explaining Priority-Action Consistency

Our model, as set forth in chapter 2, posits three factors that help us to understand the extent and circumstances under which clergywomen may be mobilized for politics. These three factors include personal principles —one's own sense of the things that are normatively desirable and proper; organizational pressure—the effect of the demands and desires inherent in the groups to which one might belong or work; and politics— the idea that the events, policies, and personalities that characterize a community will affect the political choices available to the citizens who reside within that community. We now apply the three elements of this model to the puzzle of priority-action consistency and inconsistency.

Principles

As James Guth and colleagues note, clergy are part of religious traditions with rich histories and unique theological doctrines.[11] Specific religious traditions socialize clergy in different ways through denomination-specific seminaries, annual denominational conferences, and official publications.[12] The socialization experiences that clergywomen undergo in their religious traditions inculcate key religiopolitical principles within them. Such principles may encourage them to engage in political activity to address their own personal political priorities. Indeed most of the women we interviewed who do take action to tackle their top political priorities noted that their religious backgrounds are steeped in traditions that often mandate political action. As one rabbi explains, "The [religious] movement that I am a part of . . . is very much in the forefront of social justice issues, sympathetic to participating in programs." Or, as a Presbyterian pastor says, "theology dictates involvement." Several of the women noted that they first embraced this ethos of caring while attending seminary. In the words of another Presbyterian woman, "The generation that I was in seminary, it was a few years post-Vietnam. There were a lot of social action issues very much at the forefront at that time, and the seminary was very involved in that kind of thing." For some women, not only does the seminary experience raise their awareness about social issues such as poverty and discrimination, but it also promotes a desire to turn that awareness into political action.

Another example of the importance of principles for priority-action consistency is the fact that several of the women believe that their status as female clergy holds them to a special political responsibility, particularly when it comes to discrimination-related issues. As one Presbyterian minister notes:

> Clergywomen have a special responsibility to articulate their politics in particular ways because we stand on the shoulders [of those] who have stood before us. Women who are ordained are here not only because of a calling from God, but [also] because of a hard-fought struggle of those who have come before us. Do I feel that women clergy have a special responsibility to articulate where we are and how we are because of those who have come before us? Yes. I mean, just because of our own embodied selves, we make a political statement whether we want to or not. . . . So, by my own embodiment, I make a political statement, about scripture, about the world, about how I understand how God works in life.

These ideas are echoed by a rabbi who says, "Because of who I am, I am reminded that I cannot be just part of the status quo on some issues. I think because of a lot of things that I have achieved, the congregation will follow me when I do political activities, because they know my involvement is well thought out." These observations reveal the importance of a principle that stresses that it is incumbent upon clergywomen, because of their minority professional status, to act on particular issues. In these instances, gender-based principles further empower clergywomen to tackle their own political priorities.

It is perhaps surprising to observe, in the results shown in table 5.4, that this sort of issue mobilization based on principles appears to be operating approximately equally for discrimination issues and for economic justice. This finding suggests that the women may not be as constrained as one might suspect from engaging in action to address discrimination, despite the controversy that marks this area of discourse, and despite the limitations they might be expected to feel as a professional minority.

Organizational Pressure

The organizations with which people are affiliated often exert direct and indirect pressure to engage in political activity, especially surrounding certain issues.[13] For clergywomen, this pressure comes primarily from the religious traditions and congregations in which they work. Organizational pressure might lead to more action than interest on the issues that their religious traditions and congregations emphasize. Women clergy may feel pressured—or, to put it more politely, encouraged—to act on such issues even if the issues do not rank among their own personal priorities. This dynamic is exemplified by the words of a minister who spends a great deal of time on political activities designed to address poverty: "My denomination has a commitment to those who are marginalized. That is something they talk about being and doing, and because of that, I am motivated to be helping people who are poor and alienated."

Organizational pressure accounts for the fact that religious factors beyond personal commitment motivate political action. Another influence on many of the women who display priority-action consistency would be supportive religious traditions and congregations that expect their clergy to be politically engaged.[14] In these cases, the women are not merely mobilized by their own personal political concerns; they are also mobilized or empowered by the organizational structures within which they work every day. Religious institutions provide women not only with spiritual advice but also with "a support system, networks, and resources," as one United Methodist minister recounts.

Most of the women who act on their own priorities work in churches or synagogues with a long history of activism in social and political causes. Many are involved in the sociopolitical programs of their congregations, which are as wide-ranging as Habitat for Humanity, soup kitchens, food pantries, homeless shelters, shelters for battered women and refugees, Head Start, low-cost day care, and after-school centers. Having such programs already established in their congregations allows many of the women easier access to opportunities for political engagement. Similar organizational mobilization occurs via denominational policy efforts that always need volunteers and leaders. A United Methodist minister mentions how she has become politically and socially engaged in gay rights issues through her denomination: "I have been involved in discussion about gay and lesbian rights. . . . My conference within the [United Methodist Church] put together a task force on implications of gay and lesbian rights, and I was the leader of the task force."

Further, several of the women, including this Presbyterian minister, note that their congregations actively encourage political participation by their clergy: "This congregation really presents its ethos of caring for God's children to the world. . . . It has clearly given me permission to articulate those things that I find important and valuable and those things that I have been involved in. I have found a wide berth at this congregation." For this minister and several others, the examples set by individual congregation members (who are often deeply involved in social and political concerns on their own) offer a base of support for their own political efforts.

The congregation can have additional effects on women clergy's decisions about political engagement. For example, several of the women we interviewed are active on discrimination-related issues in part because of the membership of their congregations. One Disciples of Christ pastor notes that her "congregation is made up of a significant number of gay and lesbian individuals. . . . This is a church that is not only diverse in [sexual] orientation, but also racially diverse." The diversity in her congregation leads this minister to become engaged in political issues concerning racism and discrimination against homosexuals. Instead of being controversial, her engagement is expected by the people she serves.

Organizational pressures are also at work for clergywomen whose action agendas do not match their priorities. A few of the women who undertake action on economic justice even though they personally do not prioritize this issue area say they are motivated to act because their religious traditions encourage it. However, most of these women are involved primarily through long-established sociopolitical programs in their own congregations. Several of the women noted that the constraint of time prompts their willingness to involve themselves in such congregational programs, even though the issues addressed by the programs may not rank among their own top political priorities. One senior United Methodist pastor acknowledges that while she would love to get involved in action on discrimination-related issues (her true passion), her senior position in the church limits the amount of time she can spend on politics. Instead, she participates in a social outreach program that her church runs to feed the homeless. She does so because the program is already well established and requires little of her time. This theme was echoed by several of the women, including a United Methodist minister who says that, as a mother, she struggles to find "a balance between family and church responsibilities." Participating in projects in which the church is already involved allows her more time at home with her children, while still affording her the opportunity to participate in a limited capacity.

Because most mainline Protestant churches and Jewish synagogues often have a long history of social outreach programs, particularly in inner cities,[15] congregational pressure for clergy to participate in such programs is often high. Even clergy with little personal desire to participate in politics sometimes become involved in these programs. One Methodist minister, whose congregation is deeply involved in a citywide, ecumenical economic-development organization as well as Habitat for Humanity, participates in these programs because "there was already a core group of people that were volunteering [once I arrived at this church] so I just help support that." She notes that, otherwise, she really has "little interest in politics, especially in this city. . . . I have been here just a year and have been so involved in making this transition; I do not have the connection in this community to be political. And it has not been one of my priorities." Two other ministers repeated this theme, including a self-professed "nonpolitical" Disciples of Christ pastor who worked with her congregation's established homeless shelter, as well as a self-described "behind-the-scenes" Baptist minister who joins along with economic programs that are run by her congregation.

Whereas organizations sometimes encourage political activism surrounding a particular set of issues, pressure may also be exerted against taking action. For any number of reasons, an organization may wish to maintain a culture of silence on particularly touchy issues. When clergywomen say they are concerned about issues that are perceived as controversial within their congregation or denomination, yet fail to take action, this organizational pressure against action should be suspected. For example, one pro-choice woman minister told us quite bluntly that she is hesitant to become involved in abortion politics because her congregation "holds a different view on abortion."

Gender may play a role in this mechanism as well. Women clergy may feel additional sensitivity to pressures that encourage them either to conform to congregational standards or to focus their energies only on core professional tasks. For example, one recently appointed woman minister noted that her congregation's previous reaction to women clergy was limiting her ability to be active in politics: "There has been only one other woman, and bless her heart, she wasn't too well received. So I have some self-imposed restrictions [on political activity]." This felt need to respond to congregational pressures may also mean that there is little time left for political action. One of the clergywomen we interviewed argued that women in general have less time to participate in politics because they must work harder than their male colleagues in order to prove themselves: "It is still true that women have to do a better job than men do, so women tend to spend more time with church activities and might not have as much time to participate in politics."

Most of the women clergy who were not willing to take action on discrimination-related issues noted that the potential responses of their congregations factored into their decisions. In the words of one Disciples of Christ minister, "One must be careful and pretty neutral, because you can make enemies pretty easily." Or, as an Episcopal priest indicated, "I have taken the political bumper stickers off my car, because I feel I have to remain neutral. Being vocal is one way to alienate a faction of the church. . . . I am nervous if [an issue] is controversial and overtly political. Conflict is uncomfortable." One United Methodist minister attributes her decision not to tackle certain political issues, despite her strong personal concern, to the wishes of her congregation: "This congregation has made a deliberate choice not to be involved in social or political involvement." Noting that her congregation is politically diverse, she has chosen to "avoid the conflicts that would emerge because of diversity to focus [instead] on spiritual development." In this sense, congregations can effectively prevent the women from taking action on political issues that concern them.

Time emerges as a critical factor for several of the clergywomen. Although many express personal concerns about discrimination, a lack of time results in two different outcomes. Some women are forced to concentrate exclusively on the most immediate needs of their congregations. Witness this Presbyterian minister: "I've got my hands full with this congregation, [so] I can't see myself heavily involved in politics." As discussed above, other women with time constraints avoid working on discrimination-related issues and instead focus on congregational programs designed to fight economic injustice. Such is the case for this United Methodist minister who works in a very large congregation: "The sad thing about being a local pastor is that I find that the amount of time that I have to be involved in [political] activities is really, really limited, especially with a congregation this size." She has time to participate only in the various social programs run by her church that are geared toward the poor and homeless. And gender may play a role in shaping time constraints. As one United Methodist minister notes, "Women clergy have a tendency to overcommit, and [we] are not good at saying no."

In light of the minority status of women clergy, the difficulty they encounter in attaining prestigious congregational appointments, and the challenges they face earning respect and authority in the pulpit, it is surprising to find that relatively few women limit their political activity because they fear alienating their congregations. It is even more surprising given the numerical decline in the membership rolls of mainline Protestantism and Judaism. With members already leaving at what some might call alarming rates, it would make sense for mainline Protestant and Jewish clergy of both genders to take steps to retain the congregation members they have rather than potentially alienating them by pursuing controversial political action. Frankly, given the fact that many of the women we interviewed serve in shrinking congregations, we were surprised that a relatively large proportion of them are willing to take on political issues that could potentially alienate parishioners.[16] Although a few women do explain that they limit their action on discrimination to preempt congregational objection, a majority of women clergy who are concerned about discrimination-related issues do not restrain themselves from taking action.

Politics

Clergy work long hours and frequently have a strong commitment to their occupation. They are often too busy to pursue political action unless an outside party makes it easy for them to do so. Recruitment from the outside political world is therefore a highly plausible explanation for the type of inconsistency displayed in the fourth row of table 5.4. It begins to answer the question of why some women act on issues that they do not list among their highest personal priorities. When they take political action on low-priority issues, they most likely do so thanks to opportunities they encounter directly at work. Quite simply, some issues are easier than others to act upon, especially when someone offers a ready opportunity to become involved.

Women clergy encounter a wide range of individuals, groups, and networks in the course of their day-to-day professional lives. With whom are they most likely to be in contact? Who is most likely to recruit them? Which organizations are easiest for them to join? Family life is also relevant to the recruitment factor. Women with children, for instance, might have less available time to take action on the political issues that concern them most, so they might opt instead to get involved in political activities that are easily accessible in their communities, regardless of their substantive content. From a different perspective, parents of school-age children often join the social networks that stem from local schools, and such networks can provide information and resources that might facilitate participation in politics of a particular variety.

In addition to denominational mobilization, individuals and groups from the community may recruit women clergy for political action. Overt mobilization by the ecumenical groups that are often found in urban environments, for example, facilitates some women's entry into the political arena.[17] An Episcopal priest recounts her experience: "A couple of years ago, I was drawn to the fact that this city had a growing population of Hispanic people. . . . Through a friendship with a nun, I became a part of the development committee for the Hispanic Education Center, and I spent a fair amount of time with that. . . . I tend to be one of those people who gets invited to [join] something that is trying to get off the ground, and I'm willing to do that."

Some women have encountered opportunities through their ministerial positions to serve as board members for organizations such as the Urban League or the United Way, which do not have explicit religious connections. Several of the women have been appointed to mayoral clergy boards or other governmental advisory councils as well. Other women are mobilized for politics by more loosely knit groups. For instance, one Disciples minister notes: "The downtown clergy try to get together pretty frequently to talk about what is going on." In each of these cases, professional ties have given clergywomen political opportunities to address the issues about which they express concern.

These clergy's status as women also yields some unique political opportunities. For instance, a rabbi who serves at an influential synagogue says that she is often invited to participate in political events that interest her due to her status as a female. She says: "Being a woman has been helpful in terms of leadership positions. . . . Since I was one of the first female rabbis ordained as a Conservative rabbi, particularly one in a very visible congregation, I feel I am often placed on denominational committees, a fairly prestigious position." Further, several of the other women we interviewed claim that gender offers outlets for political participation that might not be available to male clergy, particularly in arenas dealing with discrimination issues. As one Presbyterian minister recounts: "Gender opens areas of compassion. . . . People will tell me stories about how they have been discriminated against racially or other problems that they have had, and they need a listening ear, I think." In turn, hearing such stories has made discrimination a top political priority for this minister, and it has also prompted her to take action to fight it.

The physical location of the woman's church or synagogue may also affect her political behavior.[18] As urban ministers who often work in economically depressed, majority-minority neighborhoods, several of the women engage in action geared at both economic development and fighting racism. As one Disciples of Christ minister states, "[It affects] you when you know white police officers shoot African Americans down the street from the church." Her participation in efforts to improve race relations is inspired in part by the difficult experiences members of her majority-black congregation face in their economically disadvantaged neighborhood.

Conclusion

It is important to note that the three explanatory factors discussed in our consideration of priority-action consistency are not mutually exclusive. Principles alone can sometimes be enough to stimulate women clergy to tackle their top political priorities. However, our evidence shows that a wide variety of factors work in the lives of these women to enable and encourage them to pursue political involvement. Some women have the organizational benefit of an accommodating or even encouraging congregation. Many belong to religious traditions that support and sometimes expect their involvement. And quite a few women encounter special recruitment opportunities because of their gender. In fact, many boards and organizations in the broader political community seek out women clergy.

These factors and many more combine to create a fluid world of political opportunities and choices for women clergy. After all, recent research on political participation has demonstrated time and again that contextual factors can play just as important a role in stimulating an individual to act politically as their own preferences and attitudes.[19] In some instances, of course, multiple factors affect women clergy's political choices. Meanwhile, women clergy might encounter cross-pressures that pull them simultaneously toward and away from acting on various issues. Their political orientations are shaped by the world of religious work in which they dwell each day.

The operation of these different factors will affect the extent to which there is consistency (or inconsistency) between clergywomen's prioritization of an issue and their willingness to pursue action to tackle it. A woman with very strong issue concerns may be more visibly affected by organizational pressure to act—and perhaps less likely to cave to organizational pressure to abstain from acting. When either organizational pressure or recruitment by the broader political community is at work, we see more action than interest on a particular issue, except when the organizational pressure is negative.

Women clergy must decide for themselves whether their own concern about an issue outstrips their fear of alienating their congregations. In any case, our findings imply that women clergy are not completely constrained by their status as a professional minority and that the religious organizational setting spurs some to pursue political action, even to address controversial and potentially divisive issues.

6
Clergywomen's Political Strategies

Any time an individual wishes to become involved in politics, he or she may choose from a wide variety of specific activities, or strategies. Women clergy employ many such strategies when they translate their social justice mission into political action. And, as we noted in chapter 2, the range of activities that we define as political is quite broad. To make sense of the range of political activities available to clergywomen, we examine two dimensions of their political strategies: *where* they take political action and *how* they do so.

The first distinction divides activities into two categories: (1) those conducted within the congregation and designed primarily to influence congregants' political attitudes and behaviors, and (2) those that directly involve the process of resource allocation or value enforcement. James Guth and colleagues identify the first type of action as *cue giving* and the second as *direct action*.[1] A clergywoman who chooses cue-giving strategies must decide how she will use her teaching and leadership authority within her congregation. To what extent will she use the pulpit or other congregational forums to teach and encourage others to fulfill the demands of the social justice mission? How do principles and pressures shape her decisions? Direct action, on the other hand, most often is geared toward the world outside of the congregation. The distinction between cue giving and direct action spotlights the diverse ways in which clergywomen seek to balance prophetic teaching, organizational leadership, pastoral care, and community involvement.

Determining where politics fits among all the other demands of being a clergyperson necessitates introspective decision making about whether one's appropriate role is to act, to inspire others to act, or both. And at the end of this decision-making process there is still the matter of choosing specific political actions to undertake. We divide clergywomen's direct-action strategies into four categories, based on their relationship to government.[2] These include:

- Electoral strategies
- Advocacy strategies
- Partnership strategies
- Gap-filling strategies

Electoral strategies include activities that revolve around elections, such as campaigning, running for office, and contributing money to candidates. When they engage in electoral activities, clergywomen influence collective decisions by affecting the selection of individuals who will make policy. *Advocacy* strategies include protesting, contacting officials, and forming congregational study groups about issues. Such activities are designed to shape collective decisions by influencing government officials or public opinion apropos of some issue. *Partnership* strategies involve working with a government entity to address a problem or provide a service. Examples of partnership activities would include serving on a community-development corporation board that receives government funding or being part of a mayoral task force. The partnership options that are available to clergy continue to expand as government officials from the White House to city hall increasingly turn to faith-based initiatives in addressing social problems. Finally, *gap filling* means working within the community to influence the distribution of resources or the enforcement of values directly—without government assistance. These actions "fill in gaps" by offering services that government does not adequately provide. A rabbi working in a soup kitchen, for example, changes the distribution of healthy food in her community, and a minister walking the streets to talk with gang members changes the enforcement of values in her community. Such activities serve members of the community, not just members of the congregation, meaning that the clergywomen can bring about change that goes beyond their congregations. In this study, we focus only on gap-filling activities that serve the broader community, not those geared specifically at certain congregation members, such as youth ministries or pastoral counseling.[3]

Upon what *principles* do these women draw as they choose their political strategies? What *pressures* do they face from their religious institutions to adopt or avoid particular strategies? How do current *political* situations influence their choices? In the interviews, clergywomen tell us which activities they see as appropriate (based on their principles) and describe the congregational or denominational pressures that shape their choices. Some also discuss how they see their political actions as responses to the political realities around them. Complementing the interview data, the national survey includes questions that ask clergy whether they approve of other clergy who engage in specific political activities and whether they have engaged in each of these activities themselves in the past year. Consequently, the survey data provide useful information about the strategies that clergy see as appropriate (again, based on their principles) and which strategies they actually employ (which shows how their principles interact with pressures and politics to create action).

Before we turn to the clergywomen's political strategies in detail, it is important to realize that two noteworthy political differences separate the four-city sample and the national sample. First, the national survey was conducted during a presidential election year, whereas the four-city study took place during a summer of few elections, save some off-year local races and a few congressional primaries. Second, urban clergywomen comprise only 26 percent of the national sample.[4] We should expect that this urban subsample would have a density of political activity surrounding them that would be similar to the four-city sample. However, 40 percent of the national sample consists of women in rural and small-town areas, where we would expect to find a much lower concentration of nonprofit and political organizations.[5]

Cue-Giving Strategies

Clergywomen who consider cue-giving strategies acknowledge that such strategies can be highly effective thanks to the authority conveyed by the pulpit. In fact, this authority gives some women pause about pursuing cue giving. As one rabbi explains, "There is enormous power associated with the pulpit. I have people come up to me who say that they remember what I said about something that I had forgotten. People are listening to what you say." The priest of a prestigious Episcopalian congregation expresses even more explicit reservations: "My congregation has put a level of trust [in me] and has given me the privilege of the pulpit in a very visible high-profile place. I would not abuse that privilege by advocating from the pulpit for any political cause." However, like other women who initially say that they do not discuss "politics" from the pulpit, she admits that she's "never hesitated to speak on issues of justice." Several women make a similar distinction between "political statements" versus "issue statements" or "Gospel messages." A Baptist explains, "Yes, I am political, but only to the extent that the Gospel insists that radically everything needs to be changed." A Conservative rabbi notes, "We try not to speak partisan politics from the pulpit, but we do make issues from the pulpit."

Several clergywomen declare that explicitly partisan political statements, especially those that endorse a particular candidate, are clearly out of bounds. One woman explains, "I do not endorse candidates from the pulpit or in church. It is both a violation of my principles regarding the separation of church and state, plus it is illegal and violates our tax-exempt status." A rabbi adds, "I don't think we should be partisan politicians from the pulpit, advocating candidates or particular parties from the pulpit. That is beyond what clergy should be doing."

Two key principles concerning cue giving emerge here. First, some women clearly distinguish between the cues that they can offer from the pulpit and other cue-giving activities, noting that the pulpit must be used with special care. Second, the women see partisan cue giving as inappropriate and even illegal—while at the same time viewing interpretation of scripture's justice messages as one of their most important responsibilities. In terms of strategy, they see advocacy-related cue giving as appropriate and even required, whereas electoral cue giving, especially from the pulpit, is inappropriate. The social justice tradition demands that the teaching of the Gospel include lessons about justice. Again and again the women told us of the powerful imperative they felt to address justice issues—and of their desire to be faithful to the radical nature of the Gospel.

Clergy do have other options outside of the pulpit for the provision of political cues, but many of the same qualifications and concerns constrain the women's decisions about utilizing such options. In the interviews the clergywomen repeatedly clarified the difference in their minds between "politics," which they often considered inappropriate, and "justice," "morality," "public affairs," and "community involvement," which they perceived as appropriate. Women say they wish to be seen considering multiple political perspectives so as to inspire their congregants to do the same. They also emphasize the importance of not coming across in an identifiably partisan fashion as well as the imperative of not alienating congregants. A Lutheran minister told us that one of the other ministers in her church pressures her to make antiabortion statements. She says she refuses to do so because she thinks it is important not to alienate anyone who might need her guidance in dealing with an unplanned pregnancy. One of her key ministry tasks is teaching confirmation classes, so she often bonds with adolescent girls. She explains, "They need to know that they can talk to me no matter what happens and no matter what the issue." This woman's principles (avoiding advocacy cue giving that might jeopardize ministerial relationships) prevent her from capitulating to her colleague's pressure to denounce abortion. As another woman observes, "As a pastor I have a responsibility for all of the people in my parish, and if I take too strong of a position on one issue, then I'm afraid I will cut off communication with them."

Further evidence of the integration of political cue giving into ministerial relationships emerges from a Methodist minister's description of her non-pulpit cue-giving opportunities: "I have a group of old men [whom] I eat lunch with on Fridays at the café here, and I think one of the reasons that I was [invited] to go there is to provide an opposing point of view." This same woman emphasizes the influence she believes she has with young people in her church: "I have a whole youth group of kids that I have managed to help, I don't know, broaden their perspective on peace and justice." Another Methodist minister shows how she translates her principles into practice for cue-giving action, even in an environment in which her congregation might not be so supportive:

[In front of the congregation] . . . you have to be more careful because there are a lot of "hot" words, and if you say them, like the word "peace," the congregation just tunes out. . . . But there are other ways that you can [talk about peace and poverty]. Like in prayers. Praying for people that we do not know and praying for, lifting up concerns that if you were talking with one of the parishioners, they might say, well, it is their own fault for being poor, for being lazy, or whatever. Making them pray for people, there is a lot of power there for teaching and how people change their worldview, and I think that that is essential.

This woman's use of public prayer to convey a political message to a congregation with much more conservative views illustrates how she is able to remain true to her principles while also responding to the realities of congregational politics.

The surveys given to the four-city sample and the national sample both include questions that ask whether clergywomen approve of various political strategies in the abstract and whether they actually used each strategy in the past year. Table 6.1 shows levels of approval and usage of various cue-giving activities. The first column examines approval and usage among women from the four-city study. Women clergy in the four cities largely approve of taking a political stand from the pulpit (78 percent) and preaching a sermon on a controversial topic (69 percent), although they do not approve of more partisan cue-giving activities such as endorsing a candidate (6 percent). There is also widespread approval (78 percent) for non-pulpit cue giving in the form of organizing study groups. No doubt even more clergy would approve of encouraging someone else in the congregation to organize a study group on a political topic, a cue-giving option that was not listed in the surveys. The third column of table 6.1 displays corresponding data from the national sample. Very few differences between the two samples emerge in terms of basic principles.

Table 6.1 also displays the percentages of clergywomen who report using each strategy in the past year (1997–98 for the urban women; 1999–2000 for the national sample). Again both samples share the same basic pattern. A very small number had endorsed candidates from the pulpit.

Table 6.1 Approval and Use of Cue-Giving Strategies

Strategy	Urban Sample		National Sample	
	Approve of strategy (Percentage)	Used strategy (Percentage)	Approve of strategy (Percentage)	Used strategy (Percentage)
Endorsed a candidate from the pulpit	6	2	—	2
Took a public stand from the pulpit	78	43	83*	29*
Gave a complete sermon on a political or controversial topic	69	39	74*	18*
Organized a study group in congregation to discuss public affairs	78	22	88*	15*

Sources: Compiled by authors from interviews; Cooperative Clergy Project 2000.

Note: The two surveys did not include questions on every activity listed above, so data is not available for some activities.

*Indicates a statistically significant difference between mainline Protestant clergywomen and clergymen with respect to approval or use of cue-giving strategies. In all cases, women were more likely than their male counterparts to approve of or use the indicated strategies. For more discussion, see Deckman et al. (2003).

A few more women had organized study groups. A larger number, but still less than half, had provided cues by taking stands from the pulpit or giving entire sermons on a political topic. In another study employing the national data, we examine differences among clergywomen and clergymen in mainline Protestant denominations and find that women are more likely than their male counterparts to approve of such cue-giving strategies *and* use them (such differences are denoted by the asterisks in table 6.1).[6]

Women are more likely to approve of cue-giving strategies than they are to use them (men clergy also share in this pattern, according to our analysis of the national data on clergymen, which is not reported here). Because one would be hard-pressed to argue that the politics of 1998 or 2000 provided no entrée for discussion of social justice issues within study groups, the gap between approval and usage of this strategy must be explained by pressure. Repeatedly the women in the interviews discuss time pressures. Lack of time may be the reason that relatively few women organize study groups to discuss public affairs, despite the fact that this option provides a means of advocacy cue giving without risking abuse of the pulpit. But it takes more time to organize a study group than it does to mention an issue from the pulpit or even to give a complete sermon on a controversial issue.

Time pressures do not help us interpret the gap between approval and usage for taking a stand from the pulpit and giving a sermon on a controversial topic. Clergy must write and deliver sermons anyway. Inserting a political message takes more time only if they feel the need to spend time keeping abreast of political issues in order to do so. However, there are many issues, such as poverty and HIV/AIDS, that may be addressed without reference to specific political news stories. The approval-usage gaps we observe for taking a public stand and giving a complete sermon make most sense if they are understood in terms of demobilizing organizational pressure. Two kinds of organizational pressure that may demobilize women from both activities stand out from the interviews: fear of losing one's job or leadership authority and fear of alienating congregants with different political views. The picture for the women in the national sample suggests a similar story, as we observe high levels of approval for the various cue-giving strategies and lower rates of actual usage.

Direct-Action Strategies

Whereas cue giving engages clergy in politics through activities designed to inform and mobilize members of the congregation, direct action places clergy right in the heart of the political process. Clergy may participate in direct action using any of the four strategy types outlined above (electoral, advocacy, partnership, and gap filling). They may undertake such activities through their congregation, or they may choose to work outside of the congregation. For example, a rabbi might engage in gap filling either through a synagogue clothing drive or by volunteering at a local shelter to provide counseling to victims of domestic violence. Even though direct action can occur via congregational programs, it does not usually flow from the day-to-day responsibilities of ministry as easily as cue-giving activities. Direct action is likely to require extra time and attention above and beyond what is spent on the core tasks of worship, education, and visitation, so it would be highly susceptible to time-crunch pressures. A quick sweep across all of the approval and action tables in this chapter suggests as much, because we see consistently larger gaps between approval and usage of direct-action strategies. To understand the lessons about political mobilization that lie behind these gaps, we again use our interview and survey data to see how clergy-women translate their social justice mission into principles concerning the appropriateness of each strategy—and how these principles interact with pressures and politics to shape the women's strategy choices.

Electoral Strategies

The obvious objective of electoral activity is to influence elections or inform voters. Toward these ends, individuals may campaign for or donate money to a candidate, political action committee, or political party. Running for office, of course, would also count as an electoral activity. Yet as we have already established, many clergywomen emphasize the importance of not appearing to be involved in partisan politics. Their concerns go beyond the risk of alienating their congregations; they also worry about church-state separation and possible challenges to their congregations' tax-exempt status. For many, professional socialization has established the importance of steering clear of overtly partisan activities. One Methodist explains how her caution about church-state separation affects her choices: "I am more careful about what I say, especially regarding how I would vote as a private citizen, because I recognize that I have greater influence than what I am comfortable with. There is also the constraint of church and state, and not wanting to put the church in a precarious tax position."

Most of the clergywomen do not approve of electoral strategies beyond voting, even though such activities do not need to be made public and do not involve the explicit use of one's clerical position or congregation. The women were especially opposed to the notion of running for office. Said one woman: "I'm not going to say that clergy should all be running for public office [even though] I think for clergy to spend their lives holed up inside the church is a mistake." Another woman adds, "I don't know that I would trust a clergyperson running for office any more than I would trust anyone else. I think we have to be political, but I think the more we become involved with the bureaucracy of politics we are tainted." In fact, when we asked women during the interview to tell us about their recent political or social activities, only two discussed electoral activities. One rabbi mentioned that she had campaigned for a state legislature candidate in the last election, and an Episcopal priest said that she donated money to political candidates. Neither of these women tied their activity to a specific issue. The basic lesson about electoral strategies that emerges from the interviews is that very few clergywomen use—or even consider—these strategies.

Table 6.2 displays approval and usage of four direct electoral strategies. Although we might expect a higher level of electoral activity during a presidential election year (and thus more evidence of electoral activity in the national sample), comparing the two samples tells a different story. The levels of electoral activity in both samples are very similar. The bottom line is that women clergy engage in precious few electoral activities. Our previous work comparing men and women clergy has found similarly low electoral activity levels among clergymen, although men are more likely both to approve of running for office and to run themselves than clergywomen—albeit still in very small numbers—whereas women

Table 6.2 Approval and Use of Direct-Action Strategies

Strategy	Urban Sample		National Sample	
	Approve of strategy (Percentage)	Used strategy (Percentage)	Approve of strategy (Percentage)	Used strategy (Percentage)
Electoral				
Ran for office	43	2	50*	2*
Worked actively on a political campaign	48	9	—	7*
Endorsed candidate publicly (not from pulpit)	35	20	46*	30*
Registered voters in church	80	6	—	—
Advocacy				
Wrote letter to the editor	83	11	—	20*
Contacted public official	80	43	—	39*
Committed civil disobedience	69	9	58*	3
Protested in march	76	7	80*	12*
Signed or circulated a petition	61	30	—	50*
Took part in boycott	74	14	—	31*
Worked with neighborhood, IAF, advocacy organization	79	34	—	—

Partnership				
Crime prevention	81	10	—	11*
Economic development	82	15	—	11*
Gap Filling Crisis				
Pregnancy center	71	6	—	10
Homeless shelter/program	82	26	—	30
Housing program	88	37	—	24*
Soup kitchens/food pantry	86	50	—	46*
Domestic violence	—	—	—	39*
Children's program	—	—	—	19
Substance abuse program	—	—	—	15*
Prison ministry	—	—	—	18*

Sources: Compiled by authors from interviews; Cooperative Clergy Project 2000.

Note: The two surveys did not include questions on every activity listed above, so data is not available for some activities.

*Indicates a statistically significant difference between mainline Protestant clergywomen and clergymen with respect to approval or use of direct-action strategies. In most cases, clergywomen were more likely than their male counterparts to approve of or use the indicated strategies. Clergymen were more likely to approve of running for office and more likely to run for office and engage in crime prevention programs, housing programs, soup kitchen/food pantry work, and prison ministries. For more discussion, see Deckman et al. (2003).

are more likely to approve of and engage in working for campaigns and endorsing political candidates publicly.[7]

Advocacy Strategies

Whereas electoral strategies focus on influencing who serves in government, advocacy strategies focus on influencing policy, the behavior of government officials, or citizens' attitudes about issues. Usually such strategies rely primarily on providing information and exerting political pressure. At the state and local level, advocacy efforts might also involve organizing and campaigning for ballot referenda and initiatives. Indeed, advocacy strategies cover a broad range of activities. The surveys asked questions about several types of advocacy activities, and the clergy-women discuss an even broader range during the interviews. Thus gaps between approval and usage of advocacy strategies need to be interpreted in a different light than was the case for electoral strategies. Although clergywomen approve of a broad range of activities in general, one would not expect each woman to be able to pursue all, or even many, such activities at the same time. The interviews reveal that quite a few women engage in additional advocacy activities that were not listed in the survey, which makes it even less likely that individual women would be involved in even a tiny fraction of the advocacy avenues included on the surveys.

We would expect instead to find women clergy choosing advocacy avenues that fit the pressures and politics of their unique situations while allowing them to be true to their own personal interests and principles. The approval patterns we observe from the surveys tell us about the principles that guide clergy's activity and provide useful information about the kinds of activities that appear best and worst suited to the pressures and politics clergywomen encounter. However, the interviews provide richer accounts of how principles, pressures, and politics interact for advocacy strategies. When we asked women which specific political or social projects they had been involved with lately, they talked most about advocacy activity. Fully two-thirds of the women mentioned some form of advocacy.

The social justice orientation of the traditions in which these women serve naturally leads them to approve of advocacy activity. While the women tend to see partisan politics as inappropriate, speaking up on political issues—especially those framed as "justice" issues—is seen as appropriate and even imperative. As one rabbi explains, "I think we should be looking for the moral and spiritual bases for certain policies and try to understand them and try to advocate on behalf of those." A fairly new Methodist minister argues that it is necessary to speak for those who have no voice and that she would be willing to do so, but she also acknowledges that she does not relish the idea: "As clergy, we are charged with the fact that we should stand up for people who can't be spoken for. So, if I had an opportunity, then I think it would be the right thing to do. I would probably say something outside of the church. But that hasn't happened [yet]. I must admit it is not something that I was searching for . . . but I don't think I would be afraid." Her observation highlights another dimension of clergy's principles concerning advocacy: the difference between appropriate advocacy within the walls of the church or synagogue versus appropriate extra-congregational advocacy.

Table 6.2 offers data about several advocacy options. As expected, the social justice mission yields very high approval rates for most types of advocacy activities, at least among the women in the four-city study. Women in the national sample report similar approval rates for two of the forms of advocacy in the table: protesting in marches and committing civil disobedience. Unfortunately, the national survey did not inquire about approval of other forms of advocacy, although we do have measures of usage for most of these actions.

As the young Methodist woman's words above suggest, the pattern of approval for advocacy activities that we see in table 6.2 provides evidence that clergy are less approving of advocacy strategies that occur via congregational activities, such as signing and circulating petitions in the congregation (although women clergy are more likely both to approve of and to engage in most of these activities than men[8]). Writing a letter to the editor stands out as the most frequently approved strategy. Writing such a letter fits the social justice principles of witnessing and modeling ethical analysis that these clergy obviously value. Yet writing a letter to the editor also makes one's stand on a political issue not only public but also a matter of public record, which could increase organizational pressure to avoid this strategy. Such was the case for a woman who told of a tense discussion in her church after she had signed her name with the title "Rev." attached (but without identifying her congregation) to an editorial supporting gay marriage. Some members felt it was important for the congregation to discuss whether it was appropriate for her to sign the editorial, even though the name of her congregation was not revealed in the newspaper. As a Lutheran woman explained, "I think the reality for ministers is that you don't ever do anything that is totally outside of the church. If I write an op-ed piece in the paper, it will affect the church." These two women demonstrate the organizational reality that clergy's political actions reflect upon their congregations, a reality that often leads clergy to avoid controversial advocacy activities.

Clergywomen may also engage in advocacy witness by signing political advertisements in newspapers. This obviously takes much less time than composing an editorial or letter to the editor, but it still makes one's stand a matter of public record. Since the interviews in Omaha were completed in the midst of the controversy over Rev. Jimmy Creech, the United Methodist minister who had officiated at a covenant ceremony for a lesbian couple, some of the Omaha women spent time explaining their decisions about whether to sign advertisements that either supported Creech or opposed gay marriage. One woman said her congregation had voted to put its name on one of the anti-Creech advertisements. The church's senior minister asked her if she would sign the advertisement. "[I said] no, I would not, because then anyone who either is homosexual or has a homosexual family member would not feel free to come and talk to me as a pastor because I [will] have cut off that dialogue." Again we hear echoes of the principle of doing no harm to ministerial relations. One woman said that she, too, refused to sign advertisements related to the Creech case. She argued that it was inappropriate for her to do so because her congregation was deeply divided over the controversy, and "I must remember that there is unity in diversity." Here again we see the mix of principles and organizational pressures that results in self-restraint for the purposes of ministry and congregational stability. In contrast, another woman argued that it is important for her to sign her name to advertisements that express her political views, because "I want my people to know where I am." Her position emphasizes the principle of prophetic witness in spite of organizational pressure that might discourage activity.

Contacting public officials also enjoys wide approval. It is one of the most widely used advocacy options, with over 40 percent of the urban women saying that they have contacted a public official in the past year. They contact members of Congress and state legislators about upcoming votes, and they act in an ombuds role by speaking on behalf of others to resolve bureaucratic snafus. One Baptist pastor explained that she worked with the American Baptist Churches' Office of Government Relations to write a letter to the U.S. Department of Agriculture to fight reductions in government commodities grants to food pantry programs. A rabbi explained how her ombuds advocacy work for immigrants in her congregation meshes with her pastoral care ministry: "I have worked very closely with several embassies and the [U.S.] State Department when several members' cases were going through the local channels. . . . That political activity was so closely related to my ministry here. That's pastoral care to those people." The women evince a widespread acceptance of advocacy as a valid aspect of pastoral care, through activities that range from appearing for individuals in court, to accompanying people who encounter problems receiving government assistance, to helping refugees navigate the maze of bureaucratic forms and approvals. They also find it relatively easy to write letters to elected officials, especially because many of their religious traditions send them issue alerts via e-mail.

Clergy's efforts to affect commerce by applying direct pressure also fit into the advocacy category. Of all of the advocacy activities, boycotting appears to fluctuate the most according to changes in external politics, in particular the presence or absence of major boycott drives in the political environment. Only 14 percent of the urban women say they participated in a boycott in 1997–98. However, 70 percent of these women report boycotting at some point in their careers, which suggests that the 1997–98 period might not have seen much boycotting in general. Comparison of the 1998 and 2000 results further supports this interpretation; the level of boycotting in the 2000 national sample nearly doubles the level from 1997–98.

Women in the four-city sample report high levels of approval and usage of local advocacy strategies. (Women in the national sample were not asked about such activities.) They see local-level advocacy as appropriate and find venues through which to engage in it. We conceptualize local advocacy activities as encompassing work with Industrial Areas Foundation organizations, neighborhood organizations, and other local advocacy groups. In 1940 Saul Alinsky founded the Industrial Areas Foundation (IAF). His idea was to train people to reorganize and rehabilitate their own neighborhoods. Since IAF's inception, faith-based organizations (such as churches and synagogues) have been key players in the foundation. Other IAF-like organizing networks have also emerged, such as the Gamaliel Foundation, which is based in Chicago. IAF and similar networks foster coalitions of congregations that approach politics from a community empowerment model.[9] The IAF-like coalitions in the four cities we studied include Omaha Together One Community (OTOC), People of Indianapolis Seeking Economic Development (POISED), Milwaukee Innercity Congregations Allied for Hope (MICAH), and the Washington Interfaith Network (WIN). Although these are well-known organizations, only seven of the women we interviewed said they were involved with them. This relative lack of involvement may stem from the confrontational tactics that the groups sometimes use, or it may be due to concerns about the personalities and approaches of a specific coalition. More of the urban women report working with neighborhood associations and other advocacy organizations, which are often less confrontational and controversial. Five of the Omaha women work with a state-level advocacy organization (Nebraskans Against the Death Penalty). During the interviews we rarely heard women discuss activism with national advocacy organizations other than those sponsored by their religious tradition.

Denominationally sponsored advocacy activity was quite common among the women we interviewed. Most of the denominational activities that the clergywomen mention address racism, but others deal with abortion, gender equality, and hunger issues. Such groups are likely to be grounded in principles that the women, as elites in the denominational organization, share. As clergy, the women are also likely to receive information and encouragement (organizational pressure) to join denomination-wide efforts. Moreover, an effort sponsored by the denomination may provide some cover for clergy whose congregations want them to avoid political advocacy. The emphasis of so many of these denominationally sponsored groups on the issue of racism reveals an interesting intersection of external and internal politics. Of all the possible social justice concerns they could target, racism is perhaps most attractive because it is an issue of concern within both the denomination and society at large (this would also be the case for gay rights). The issue of racism hits home for Protestant denominations, which struggle continually with the challenge of integrating racial minorities into their often all-white congregations.

Five of the women told us they employ the advocacy strategy of keeping tabs on the implementation of a particular policy. In Milwaukee, clergywomen explained that they followed Wisconsin's controversial welfare-to-work and school-choice initiatives. One Indianapolis woman said she is part of a group of Episcopal and Lutheran ministers who had been meeting regularly to discuss that city's schools. Indianapolis has a school-choice policy in place as well, and these ministers were concerned about the effects of that policy on inner-city schools. These examples of policy monitoring clearly demonstrate the impact of political context. Many of the women focus their attention on specific issues, such as welfare reform and education, because the issues are highly charged in the cities where they live and work.

Another Indianapolis woman told us about her involvement with an ad hoc group of downtown clergy who had just begun meeting to research homelessness in the city. Her involvement with this group again highlights the role of political context. Homelessness literally came to the congregations' doorsteps: "All of us have noticed in the last month a significant growth in the number of people asking for assistance. . . . Is it because they can only be on welfare for six months and now it is over? Or [is it] the job market? . . . We are trying to find out the cause." This clergy group decided to conduct research to discover what was causing the problem before moving on to other forms of advocacy to address it.

A few women also mentioned participating in prayer vigils organized in response to violence in their community. Two Indianapolis women participated in antiviolence prayer vigils sponsored by an interdenominational religious group (the Greater Indianapolis Church Federation). In all four cities, clergy and laity meet regularly to pray at sites where people have been murdered. These vigils serve as advocacy because they bring attention to the problem of violence, call the community to a shared sense of responsibility, and embolden people to stand against evil, as embodied in a social issue such as crime. Moreover, prayers for divine assistance in changing attitudes, behaviors, and policies fit the advocacy mode of activism very well.

Partnership Strategies

We now turn to partnership activities, which means that we move from efforts to influence policy through persuasion toward attempts to influence policy through implementation. Partnership finds clergy working with government agencies to achieve some policy goal. Clergy can work through their congregations in partnership activity. For example, a minister may administrate a social service program in her church or synagogue that receives funds through the Charitable Choice provision of federal welfare law. Efforts by the presidential administration of George W. Bush and state and local officials to open doors to deeper partnerships between government and faith-based organizations may well pave the way for more clergy involvement in congregation-based partnership activity.[10] Clergy may also engage in partnership activities through work with other nongovernmental organizations, be they religious or secular. For example, a rabbi might serve on the board of a community-development corporation that works to secure government funding. A minister might work with a religious-based social service agency such as Lutheran Social Services. Clergy are also sometimes asked to participate individually in partnership with government through clergy task forces or racial reconciliation networks. Volunteer efforts by individual clergy to work with crime-watch groups or to support public school programs would also qualify as partnership strategies.

Partnership activities tend to take place at the local level and focus on policy implementation and problem solving. Table 6.2 shows the patterns of approval and usage of two partnership strategies among the women we interviewed. Unfortunately, the national survey did not ask whether clergy approve of either partnership or gap-filling actions, but we do have national data on usage of these two sets of strategies. The pattern that stands out most clearly in table 6.2 with regard to partnership is the large gap between approval and usage. For the most part, clergy approve of working in partnership with government. Gone is the concern about church-state issues that dominates the women's discussions of electoral activities: more than 80 percent of the clergy appear to have no problem with the idea of clergy working closely with government to deliver services or tackle local problems such as crime and racism. Nevertheless, actual levels of activity are quite low. Fewer than 20 percent of the women in either study report engaging in partnership activities for community development and crime prevention—areas where longstanding community-development corporations and crime-watch organizations should facilitate partnership. We found in another study that male clergy were more likely to engage in crime prevention programs, whereas women were more likely to take part in community development.[11]

Six distinct types of partnership activities emerge from the interview responses. These include participation in community-development corporation boards and social service centers (both nonprofit entities that receive significant government funding), school partnerships, public housing programs, mayoral clergy advisory boards, and other government committees. The women mention community-development corporation boards most frequently, but even this form of activity is rare (fewer than ten of the women list it). The set of school partnerships illustrates the diverse ways in which clergy—as leaders in congregations, as mothers, and as citizens—join in partnership with local schools. One minister from Indianapolis works in partnership with the public schools in a program that provides activities for children on teacher in-service training days. Two of the school partnership activities fit the mother or citizenship roles: work on fund-raisers for the public school and involvement in the Parent Teacher Association. A rabbi also served on a sex-education committee for her public school district. Her clergy title may have lent legitimacy to the actions of the committee, but it did not shield her from strident opposition by others who were working on the same issue from a conservative religious viewpoint. "The religious extremists fought the rest of the committee on every issue, and there were several times when I feared for my public safety."

The most plausible culprit (other than time pressure) behind the consistently low levels of partnership activity despite high interest in such activity is the difficulty women face in entering into these partnerships. Nearly all of the partnership options require that a clergywoman be selected in order to participate. Moreover, many partnership activities offer a limited number of openings. Statutes, bylaws, funding, or mayoral staff may limit the size of the partnership body. Also noteworthy is the fact that we conducted our interviews before Charitable Choice was firmly in place and before George W. Bush was elected to the presidency. The interview data, then, provide a benchmark against which to compare clergy's levels of partnership activity in cities after the rise of faith-based initiatives. Unfortunately the 2000 survey did not ask questions of adequate specificity to allow us to measure any such growth in partnership activities.

Gap-Filling Strategies

Like partnership activities, gap-filling activities often involve clergy in the implementation of social programs. By its nature, however, gap filling does not include joint efforts with government agencies or programs. Clergy do gap-filling work through their congregations, through other organizations, or even independently. In each case, they provide social services without the assistance of government funding, government recognition, or government staff. For instance, a pastor might lead efforts to establish or run a food pantry in the congregation. A rabbi might start a mentoring program that links inner-city youth with older adults. Any such efforts by clergy to provide social services through nongovernmental means qualify as gap filling. They fill the gap that separates what government does and the extent of the community's needs.

The final section of table 6.2 reports the levels of approval and usage of various kinds of gap-filling strategies. Clergy in the national sample were not asked if they approved of gap filling, and data in the final column represent clergywomen who indicated they spent personal time on gap-filling activities. In our interviews, more than 80 percent of the clergy approve of each of the gap-filling strategies except for crisis pregnancy centers. The lower level of approval for these centers is likely due to their antiabortion emphasis, an approach that many of these women would not support. Nonetheless, more than 70 percent approve of clergy involvement in crisis pregnancy centers, but the level of participation in these centers is by far the lowest.

The highest levels of gap-filling activity for both the four-city and the national samples apply to food banks and soup kitchens. Nearly half of the women in each sample find a way to participate in these programs over the course of a year. Several women also tackle housing problems, either through local nonprofit homeless-sheltering programs or Habitat for Humanity, a nonprofit organization that works with churches to build houses with families in need of affordable housing.

The national survey asks about a longer list of gap-filling activities, so it provides a picture of some of the other ways in which clergy might fill gaps. Work with domestic violence–prevention programs stands out in this regard. About 20 percent of the women in the national sample also invest time in children's programming (child care, programs for neighborhood children, or scouting) and prison ministry.

According to our previous research,[12] it is somewhat surprising that male clergy were more likely to be involved with food pantries, which might be more stereotypically "feminine" work. Less surprising is the finding that clergymen spend more time in prison ministries and in housing programs such as Habitat for Humanity. However, women clergy are more likely than men to counsel victims of domestic violence, an issue that predominantly affects women, and to be involved with drug rehabilitation programs.

The clergywomen overwhelmingly approve of partnership and gap-filling activities, in contrast with their mixed approval of advocacy and their very low approval of electoral activities. Partnership and gap-filling activities may have the highest levels of approval because they are perceived as the least political, even though partnership activities involve working directly with government. The women's high level of approval for gap filling flows from the fact that most of these activities involve simply helping others—often those of low socioeconomic status. Such activities are clearly central elements of faithfulness to the social justice demands of the scriptures. Moreover, they carry none of the church-state stigmas and few of the partisan concerns that are commonly associated with advocacy or electoral activities.

Comparing Political Strategies

Table 6.2 reveals sweeping approval of most political strategies, with the exception of electoral activity. Not surprisingly, it also shows that electoral strategies are the least used. The women's high levels of approval of and involvement in gap filling fit our expectations. Mainline Protestants and Jews emphasize caring for "the least of them," and relatively low levels of controversy attend programs that provide direct services for the poor. We were, however, surprised by the large numbers of women who employ advocacy strategies. Women report using advocacy strategies more than any of the other strategies, including gap filling. The national data diverge here somewhat; gap filling is the most popular course of action nationally, followed by advocacy. Part of the reason for this discrepancy, however, may be methodological. As we noted earlier, in our interviews women mentioned a variety of strategies—in particular advocacy strategies—that were not included in the national survey. We suspect that if we had the ability to interview each of the women in the national sample, advocacy rates might be higher.[13]

Although all of these women serve in religious traditions that embrace modernity and have therefore legitimized organized religion's role of speaking out on contemporary political issues, it is still surprising that so many of these women say they undertake advocacy activities. Among the four types of political strategies, advocacy would seem to be the most dangerous for women clergy, who are so often concerned about job security, acceptance, and legitimacy. The fact that several of the women do their advocacy work through denominational organizations no doubt lessens the risk. Advocacy for the poor is also likely to be a relatively low-risk enterprise, as long as the clergywoman does not call for a drastic restructuring of capitalism. However, the women's advocacy activities are overwhelmingly focused upon controversial rights-related issues. Thirty-one interview accounts of advocacy activities revolve around rights—nearly triple the number of accounts of economic-related advocacy. Clearly the women do not shy away from frontline controversy; instead, they are vocal advocates for the rights of people of color, gays and lesbians, and women—despite facing some organizational pressures to eschew such issues. The stereotypical image of women clergy as fearful of acting on controversial issues because they feel their positions and status are vulnerable is simply not supported by our analysis.

Lest one assume that these clergywomen are out boldly proclaiming a gospel of social justice with no concern for the possible consequences they might face within their religious institutions, we must note that several of the women engage in advocacy in ways that would not be very visible to their congregations. Recall the story of one woman in chapter 5 who explained that she undertook AIDS advocacy "incognito" because she "hope[d] her congregation did not find out."

The Role of Political Context in Strategy Choice

In search of direct clues about the influence of political context on clergy-women's strategy choices, we now turn to an examination of differences in strategy usage among women in each of the four cities (despite small sample sizes). Different strategy options may be more or less viable in some settings than in others. For instance, one of the ministers in Indianapolis referred to her city's political climate as "highly Republican, which is not my political bent." Because she feels she has little chance of influencing conservative politicians, she finds it more effective to direct her energies beyond the purview of government and into service-provision work with nonprofit organizations.

Table 6.3 shows the percentages of women in each city who report using each of the three most common direct-action strategies (advocacy, partnership, and gap filling). Since the number of women in each city is small, we pay attention only to major differences here and recognize the need to treat these findings with caution. However, once again, the results for advocacy are striking. In conservative Omaha and Indianapolis, where one might expect clergywomen's liberal political views to be most controversial, more, not fewer, women engage in advocacy. This is true *despite* the fact that more women in Omaha report feeling gender-related constraints on their political action. These clergywomen are mobilized, not demobilized, by an unreceptive political climate. This finding is consistent with earlier research that shows urban clergy to be most politically active when they believe that they alone are in a position to help the disadvantaged.[14]

Another pattern that stands out in table 6.3 is the higher level of

Table 6.3 Strategies by City (Urban Interview Sample)

	Indianapolis (Percentage)	Milwaukee (Percentage)	Omaha (Percentage)	Washington, D.C (Percentage)
Advocacy	75	57	88	50
Partnership	50	7	31	19
Gap Filling	50	50	63	69

Sources: Compiled by authors from interviews.
Note: Figures are the percentages of women in each city who report activities that fit into each strategy.

partnership activity in Indianapolis. Political context also offers a reason for this difference. Stephen Goldsmith, who was the mayor of Indianapolis at the time of the interviews, emphasized partnerships between congregations and city government throughout his administration. He began this effort in the early 1990s—well before the birth of Charitable Choice and its attendant emphasis on partnerships between government and faith-based organizations. Thus city hall would have been creating partnership opportunities and recruiting Indianapolis clergy to fill them. Moreover, white clergy from the traditions covered in this study historically have been active in partnerships for economic development in Indianapolis.[15] A ministerial association still oversees the community-development corporation in at least one Indianapolis neighborhood. Political context and explicit efforts on the part of city government therefore combine to create a climate that increases Indianapolis clergy's ability to enter into partnership activities.

Gap-filling strategies differ least from city to city, as should be expected. Regardless of the particular governmental officials or political context in place in a given city, there is sure to be a need to assist the poor and marginalized and to provide programming options for children and senior citizens. Past research indicates that clergy who serve in neighborhoods with high poverty rates are most likely to engage in such activities,[16] which could be an explanation for the higher rates of gap filling we observe for Washington, D.C. The main lesson to emerge from the table, however, is that there are sufficient opportunities in all four cities for many clergywomen to engage in at least one gap-filling activity.

Political Strategy Choices: The National Picture

While the four-city study provides rich, grounded stories of mobilization, the small number of women in this study precludes multivariate statistical analysis. Multivariate analysis provides a different view of clergywomen's political mobilization by allowing us to examine the independent and relative influences of principles, pressures, and politics on their strategy choices. The strength of the 2000 national survey is that it yields a large enough sample to allow for multivariate analysis. However, we must bear in mind that the national data provide a narrower picture of mobilization due to the specific questions asked on the survey. We can analyze only the range of activities that were included in the survey, and we can test only for effects of the principles and pressures that it measured. Nevertheless, the similarities between the urban and national samples, as well as the measures of strategy use, pressures, and principles available from the national survey, allow us to pursue multivariate analysis.

It is important to note that the following analysis focuses on low-level mobilization. The specific question we can answer asks which factors push someone past the threshold of *inaction* to participate in at least one activity. We are not analyzing levels of mobilization per se; we do not answer the question of why some clergy are very active while others are inactive. This latter research question poses great measurement challenges that need to be tackled in future studies of clergy mobilization. Nevertheless, answering the question of which factors push someone past the threshold of inaction provides a good starting point, especially because fewer than half of the clergy pass this threshold for most of the activities measured in the survey.

We use logistic regression analysis of the 2000 survey data to assess the influence of various principles and organizational pressures on the likelihood that a minister or rabbi will cross the threshold of mobilization by actually utilizing a political strategy of which she approves. Logistic regression allows us to predict statistically whether people are likely to do something of interest or not based on independent predictor variables. Table 6.4 summarizes the results for cue-giving strategies, and table 6.5 does the same for direct-action strategies. (See appendix 6.1 for descriptions of the variables and methods.)

Table 6.4 Cue-Giving Mobilization

	DV: Took a public stand from the pulpit[a]		DV: Gave a complete sermon on a political or controversial topic[b]		DV: Organized a congregational study group to discuss public affairs[c]	
	Coeff. B	Est. odds ratio/MLE (Exp [B])	Coeff. B	Est. odds ratio/MLE (Exp [B])	Coeff. B	Est. odds ratio/MLE (Exp [B])
Principles						
Social justice belief	0.3311*	1.3925	0.6387***	1.8939	–0.1235	0.8838
Theological beliefs encourage political involvement	0.7224***	2.0594	0.8495***	2.3384	0.5829**	1.7913
Political efficacy of ministers	0.3349*	1.3979	0.2700	1.3100	0.0909	1.0951
Pressures						
Congregation encourages political involvement	0.4577*	1.5804	0.3133	1.3679	–0.1460	0.8642
Other clergy encourage political involvement	–0.6723**	0.5105	–0.3287	0.7199	0.5464**	1.7271
Activity level of congregation	0.0063	1.0063	0.0042	1.0042	0.0156**	1.0157
Urban setting	–0.4945	0.6099	–1.094***	0.3349	–0.0317	0.9688

Source: Cooperative Clergy Project 2000.

Note: Results are from multivariate logistic regression. Only significant predictors are listed. The models included all the variables listed as well as: ideology, social issues clergy–laity gap, economic issues clergy–laity gap, gender access, and gender difficulty. (See appendix 6.1 for descriptions of the variables and methods.)

*p < .10; **p < .05; ***p < .001   [a]n = 223; percent categorized correctly = 67.26%; model chi-square = 33.690; p < .001   [b]n = 369; percent categorized correctly = 85.91%; model chi-square = 41.350; p < .001   [c]n = 447; percent categorized correctly = 86.13%; model chi-square = 30.348; p < .003

Table 6.5 Direct-Action Mobilization

	DV: Electoral Activities[a]		DV: Advocacy Activities[b]		DV: Partnership Activities[c]		DV: Gap-Filling Activities[d]	
	Coeff. B	Est. Odds Ratio/MLE (Exp [B])	Coeff. B	Est. Odds Ratio/MLE (Exp [B])	Coeff. B	Est. Odds Ratio/MLE (Exp [B])	Coeff. B	Est. Odds Ratio/MLE (Exp [B])
Principles								
Social justice belief	0.0793	1.0825	0.1798	1.1970	−0.2663*	0.7662	0.0820	1.0855
Theological beliefs encourage political involvement	0.1969	1.2176	0.4770***	1.6112	−0.1729	0.8412	0.4573***	1.5799
Pressures								
Congregation encourages political involvement	0.8747**	2.3982	0.4239**	1.5278	−0.3337*	0.7163	0.0422	1.0431
Other clergy encourage political involvement	0.3584	1.4310	−0.2112	0.8096	0.3210	0.8304	−0.4184**	0.6581
Social issues (clergy-laity gap)	−0.9041*	0.4049	0.1018	1.1071	0.4158*	1.5156	0.5098**	1.6650
Activity level of congregation	0.0176	1.0178	0.0094	1.0095	0.0216***	1.0218	0.0145*	1.0146

Source: Cooperative Clergy Project 2000.

Note: Results are from multivariate logistic regression. Only significant predictors are listed. The models included all the variables listed as well as: ideology, social issues clergy-laity gap, economic issues clergy-laity gap, gender access, and gender difficulty. (See appendix 6.1 for descriptions of the variables and methods.)

*p < .10; **p < .05; ***p < .01

[a] n = 256; percent categorized correctly = 93.36%; model chi-square = 23.496; p < .05
[b] n = 410; percent categorized correctly = 69.76%; model chi-square = 31.903; p < .002
[c] n = 513; percent categorized correctly = 82.65%; model chi-square = 38.454; p < .001
[d] n = 513; percent categorized correctly = 76.80%; model chi-square = 33.305; p < .001

Cue-Giving Mobilization

The first model in table 6.4 (shown in the first column) examines which factors most powerfully predict a clergywoman's willingness to take a political stand while preaching from the pulpit. Here we find that pressures exerted by congregations and other clergy play significant roles. Women clergy whose congregations encourage them to engage in politics are more likely to preach briefly about a political issue (and conversely, those who are discouraged are less likely). On the other hand, women who are encouraged to engage in politics by other clergy are much less likely (all else being equal) to take a pulpit stand on issues. This finding shows that pressure from other clergy must emphasize political strategies other than taking pulpit stands on issues. The no-harm principle that so many women discuss in the interviews must play a role here as well; they feel they must allow for diverse views and avoid alienating members. Women clergy's strategy choices are also affected by their own personal attitudes and preferences. The more their own theological beliefs encourage involvement in politics, the more likely they are to take public, political stands.

Taking a political stand on an issue from the pulpit is one thing, but delivering an entire sermon on a controversial social or political issue is quite another. In the second model (column two of table 6.4), we find that the pressures women encounter from their congregations and other clergy are *not* statistically significant, although clergy's own theological beliefs remain a significant predictor. We also find that women who embrace the social justice mission are significantly more likely to preach on controversial issues.

We included a measure of whether or not clergywomen work in urban settings to see if this difference in political context mattered. We expected to find that the high density of political opportunities in cities might make some direct-action strategies more viable, thereby decreasing women's use of the more symbolic cue-giving strategies. The urban variable is in fact significant here, but it indicates that clergywomen who serve in cities are less likely to give a complete sermon on a political issue. This finding does not fit a density argument at all, but at the same time measures of political distance between clergy and laity (see appendix 6.1) are not significant. One would expect differences in political views on social issues to be a serious source of demobilization for cue giving. One reason for the lack of significance here is measurement error; political distance between a clergywoman and her congregation is a concept that is very difficult to measure, especially when the measure we have available is the clergywoman's self-perception of distance. We reviewed the interview data for further clues and noticed that the women frequently said they restrain themselves politically because of their congregations' political *diversity* rather than any homogeneous conservatism in the pews. Perhaps the urban variable actually captures the effect of greater congregational political diversity instead of any external political effect.

The final model in table 6.4, depicted in the last column, examines women clergy's propensity to organize congregational groups to study public issues. Encouragement by other clergy plays a significant role here; those who receive encouragement from their peers are more likely to organize study groups. Women clergy who report that their own theological beliefs encourage their engagement in politics are also more likely to organize study groups. The congregation's political activity level matters as well. Presiding over a congregation that is politically active is a significant predictor of whether women clergy organize political study groups. Having a congregation that is already active may reduce the time pressures on clergy—or at least assure clergy that the time they spend coordinating such study groups is likely to bear fruit.

The national survey did not include a measure of religious calling to politics analogous to those we use in chapter 3. However, we find strong positive results for the item that asks whether one's theology encourages political action. These results demonstrate that clergy who perceive political obligations as part of their religious mission are likely to engage in cue giving. Indeed, the principle that theology encourages political involvement stands out as one of the strongest mobilizing factors for cue-giving strategies. Commitment to the social justice mission is also significant (or nearly significant) in two of the three models. And women clergy appear to listen to their congregants. When congregational attitudes encourage clergy to be involved in politics, women clergy feel emboldened to use cue-giving strategies.

In two cases (taking a pulpit stand and organizing a congregational group), clergywomen's peers either mobilize or demobilize them. The phrase "other clergy," of course, could be taken by survey respondents to mean senior clergy within one's own congregation or religious tradition. If this is the case, then our findings might suggest that women do sometimes avoid political involvement out of fear that it could hinder their employment status. The women who are most likely to take a political stand from the pulpit (which is perhaps riskier than preaching an entire sermon that covers both sides of an issue) stand out for their evident willingness to buck this pressure. On the other hand, women who take pulpit stands might be reacting to an intensified need to bear prophetic witness because of encounters with other clergy who discourage political engagement.

Perhaps the most surprising finding concerning cue giving is that women clergy in the national study do not appear to be restraining themselves from cue-giving activities out of fear that their congregations have conflicting political views. This finding could be due to measurement problems. Or the real issue may be congregational diversity rather than political distance, as the interview data suggest. Or strong prophetic principles may push some clergywomen to step up to the challenge of cue giving.

Direct-Action Mobilization

Table 6.5 examines the impact of various principles and pressures on mobilization for direct action. Again, the models attempt to assess differences in the mobilization levels of clergy who approve of each strategy. Unlike the models presented in table 6.4, however, the direct-action models combine all of the activities listed in the survey that fit into each strategy type. So, for example, the advocacy model predicts which of the clergy who approve of advocacy strategies are likely to engage in at least one of *any* of the advocacy options listed in the survey.

As the first model in table 6.5 demonstrates, there is just one significant predictor of electoral activity. Clergy who report that their congregation encourages their involvement in politics are more likely to engage in electoral activities. Given the tricky nature of electoral activity among clergy, it is no surprise that women ministers and rabbis would pursue this kind of activity only with the blessing of their congregations. Clergy who think they have different political views from their congregations are less likely either to run for office or to campaign for political candidates. Such political action could threaten relations between a clergywoman and her flock.

The results in the second column for advocacy show that only two variables reach statistical significance. A clergywoman's decision to engage in advocacy work is related to her own theological views and the views of her congregation. Here again, perceived political distance between a clergywoman and her congregation does not predict her likelihood of using advocacy strategies. Assuming that this measure does tap into the notion of the clergy-laity gap,[17] these results suggest that political differences with congregation members do not prevent clergywomen from choosing advocacy as a strategy. The clergy-laity gap may, however, limit the women's level of activity, or it may influence which specific advocacy options they choose. It is also important to bear in mind that the survey did not ask about involvement in either the denominational or IAF groups that coordinated much of the advocacy we heard about in the interviews. Instead, the advocacy model focuses only on predicting which clergy did at least one of the following tasks in 2000: wrote a letter to the editor, contacted a public official, committed civil disobedience, participated in a protest march or boycott, or signed or circulated a petition.

An interesting shift takes place as we move from considering electoral and advocacy mobilization to partnership and gap filling. With the exception of the continuing strong mobilizing influence of personal theological beliefs in the advocacy model, many of the pressures appear to work in different ways than was the case for electoral and advocacy strategies. Although the influence is not terribly strong, having a politically active congregation emerges as a statistically significant factor for decisions about whether to engage in time-consuming partnership and gap-filling programs. Even more noteworthy is the fact that the clergy-laity gap actually serves to mobilize clergywomen for partnership and gap filling. Women, even those who face myriad demobilizing pressures, seem to see partnership and gap-filling activities as "safe." Do demobilizing pressures actually have the effect of pushing some of the women into partnership and gap-filling activities? Or might the women who prefer partnership or gap filling simply be less politically oriented? These are but two of the many questions that must be answered as scholars begin to pay more attention to partnership and gap filling as viable political strategies.

Conclusion

The emerging pattern in this chapter that varies most from our initial expectations is the clergywomen's heavy use of advocacy as a political strategy—even on controversial issues and even in conservative political climates. This surprised us because our initial hypothesis was that clergywomen would exercise tremendous caution when choosing forms of political activity, remaining especially circumspect about potentially controversial forms of advocacy. However, the women's use of advocacy is perhaps a bit less surprising in light of the amount of attention they give to controversial rights issues, as presented in the previous two chapters. Although the demobilizing pressure of the clergy-laity gap has received much attention in previous studies, we find a plethora of organizational pressures that work in the other direction to mobilize clergywomen for political action. In our examinations of both the substantive and strategic nature of women clergy's political actions, we find that they are substantially less demobilized by organizational pressures than we had expected, except when it comes to pressures exerted by other clergy. (Like everyone, clergywomen would appear to be susceptible to peer pressure!)

The limited demobilization we find among these women makes even more sense considering the influence of religion on their political choices. The Jewish and Protestant traditions both emphasize the need to be faithful despite sacrifice or persecution. Both honor the examples set by prophets who persisted in challenging leaders and fellow believers, often with unpopular messages. Consequently, we could expect clergy, male or female, to be less sensitive to demobilization dynamics than would be the case for professionals in other fields, who do not share a commitment to such a shared story of sacrifice.

Before we brush aside demobilization concerns that arise from either gender discrimination or conservative pressures from the pews, it is important to emphasize again that the political mobilization of which we write is low-level mobilization. We were concerned only with whether the clergywomen undertook *one* action out of the many possibilities available to them in each category. The fact that many organizational pressures do not appear to keep women from crossing our low mobilization threshold does not mean that the pressures do not exist, nor does it mean that organizational pressure might not prevent clergywomen from pursuing *all* of their political goals. We know from our interviews that many clergywomen are highly interested in and aware of politics, yet there are definite limits to the extent to which they are willing to transform their interest and knowledge into political action. The constraints they face may work in subtle ways that the clergywomen may not even recognize. Organizational pressures might not keep clergywomen from speaking out about controversial issues, but they may work to shape the ways in which such women choose to act on their concerns. We find evidence of this possibility in the women's emphasis on *denominational* advocacy activities, which are likely the safest available venues for their participation. On the other hand, the women may be active in denominational groups because these groups are convenient in the face of the overwhelming time pressures that all clergy face.

Appendix 6.1 Logistic Regression Methodology

The data for the logistic regressions come from the 2000 Cooperative Clergy Project. The regressions include only those clergy who approve of the political strategy being tested (except in the case of partnership and gap-filling strategies, where no approval measures exist). The statistical tests reported in tables 6.4 and 6.5 examine the effects of various principles, pressures, and politics on the likelihood that a clergywoman would use any one strategy in the previous year. In each case a logistic regression calculates the impact of each of the variables on the probability that a woman undertook a particular kind of political strategy. In the cue-giving models (table 6.4), we examine whether or not women clergy took a public stand from the pulpit, gave a sermon on a controversial topic, or organized a political study group in their congregations as the dependent variables. Because we include only those women who approve of the actions, we could not include endorsing candidates as a dependent variable, as survey respondents were not asked whether they approved of such an action.

Our independent variables reflect political views, theological beliefs, organizational pressures, and contextual factors. In terms of organizational pressures, we control for the encouragement that ministers receive from either their own congregations or other clergy. Specifically, respondents were asked (using a Likert scale) whether the attitudes of their congregation or other clergy either greatly discourage (coded as 1) or greatly encourage (coded as 5) their involvement in politics or public affairs. To account for the possible discrepancies between the political views of the clergy and their congregants, we include two "political distance" variables. Clergy were asked how their views on economic and social issues compared with the views of their congregants on a scale of 1 to 5 (where 1 is much more conservative and 5 is much more liberal; a score of 3 indicated that clergy felt their views on these issues were about the same as those of the congregation). We recoded these variables so that women who scored either a 1 or 5 (indicating the most disagreement possible with their congregants) were coded 1, while those who reported that their views were somewhat more conservative, about the same, or somewhat more liberal were coded 0.

As we have recounted throughout the book, gender accounts for other pressures that these women may face. We include two control variables to account for both the potential mobilizing influence of gender and its potentially demobilizing effect. Women were asked if they agreed with the following statements (1 = strongly disagree; 5 = strongly agree): "Because of my gender, I have easier access to opportunities to get involved in politics" and "My gender makes it more difficult for me to get involved in politics." We are interested in discovering whether or not gender emerges as a mobilizing or demobilizing force.

The controls for our regression analyses are not limited to possible organizational or gender pressures women clergy face. We also look at the women's personal and theological views. We ask women the extent to which their own theological beliefs discourage (coded as 1) or encourage (coded as 5) their political involvement. We also include a measure that asks the extent to which they agree (1 = strongly disagree; 5 = strongly agree) that social justice is at the heart of the Gospel. We account for political efficacy by controlling for respondents' belief that clergy "have a great potential to influence the political beliefs of their congregations" (1 = strongly disagree; 5 = strongly agree). Finally, we include a control for ideology, measured here on a five-point scale (1 = very liberal; 5 = very conservative).

Two other factors tap into the contexts in which women clergy find themselves. First, we control for whether a clergywoman works in an urban environment, which we define here to mean women who self-report working in cities with more than 50,000 inhabitants. Second, we take the congregation's level of activity in various sociopolitical programs into account. Clergy were asked to report the percentage of adult congregation members who were active in a variety of such programs.

In our analyses of direct-action strategies, we included only those clergy who approved of each type of strategy. In the case of electoral strategies, we use those who approve of clergy running for political office (survey respondents were not asked their approval of the other two types of electoral activities). We then created a new dependent variable in which women clergy who reported either running for office *or* working on a political campaign were coded 1, while those who did neither were coded 0. We employ the same independent variables used in the cue-giving models.

The dependent variable in the advocacy analysis is coded as 1 for women clergy who report using at least one of the advocacy strategies; those who report engaging in no advocacy activities are coded 0. To capture some essence of the approval-usage gap, we included the 80 percent of women clergy who approve of protesting in marches, suspecting that those 20 percent who do not would be less willing to support other forms of action.

The dependent variable in our partnership analysis measures whether women gave of their personal time in support of a crime-prevention or economic-development action linked to government (coded 1 for yes, 0 for no), which is slightly different from the previous two categories of direct-action strategies, in which women clergy were asked if they participated in various activities within the past year. Because the survey provides no approval measures for partnership, we include all women in this model.

The final model deals with gap-filling activities. The dependent variable codes clergywomen who indicated that they spent time in any of the eight gap-filling programs listed in table 6.2 as 1; those who reported no activity in gap-filling activities were coded as 0. We use the same independent variables in all regression analyses.

7
Prospects for the Future

Based on previous research about clergywomen's experiences, we expected to tell a depressing story in this book. We thought clergywomen's accounts of their political lives would be rife with constraint, frustration, and exclusion. Instead, we met many women clergy who do find the time and opportunity to participate in politics (at least to some extent)—and others who dedicate substantial energy to political action. These clergy are, as our book's title conveys, women with a mission—a social justice mission—that engages them in politics in both their religious institutions and beyond. Each day clergywomen undertake an array of activities to help disadvantaged, marginalized, and forgotten members of their communities. Yet these women are not immune to the challenges of navigating conservative political climates, nor are they untouched by the trials of working as women in a male-dominated profession. The ways in which gender-related factors influence their political choices remain a central element of their personal stories—and thus they have constituted a central aspect of our analysis. However, constraints are but one set of dynamics that shape the political lives of women clergy. As we have seen throughout the book, myriad forces are also at play that empower and mobilize them.

We have found that many clergywomen embrace the political world with enthusiasm, bridging the chasm between the sacred and the secular.[1] Some are called to political action outside the walls of their churches and synagogues. Others are called to make public statements on political issues. Still others prefer not to take any political action. What ties all of these women together—each in their own individual way—is an over-whelming commitment to a mission that involves fighting for justice and against discrimination. Mutually reinforcing factors ranging from per-sonal experience as an underappreciated professional minority to sociali-zation within mainline Protestantism and Judaism seem to inspire in women clergy an exceptional commitment to social justice issues. At the same time, we do find some evidence of political diversity among clergywomen. Not all see themselves as either liberal or feminist, and not all choose to pursue political activity. Yet women clergy appear to be more uniformly left leaning in their politics than is the case among their male colleagues in the same religious traditions, or among women in the American population at large. Consistent with previous studies of pro-gressive religious involvement,[2] women ministers and rabbis direct their political energies into an enormous variety of local- and state-level ef-forts. And like previous studies, this book shows that clergy are often key political leaders on the local front.[3] They assess local problems and in-habit the front lines, tackling these problems using a wide assortment of political strategies. Such is not always the stuff of sensational national political debate. But clergywomen can make a tremendous difference by working shoulder to shoulder with other local leaders to tackle the causes and consequences of homelessness or to fight racism and violence in their own cities.

As we argue throughout the book, most of the clergywomen's political priorities and actions fit squarely into a social justice mission. Above all, we have been concerned with the translation of social justice–related po-litical principles into political action, in the form of both issues tackled and strategies chosen. Our theoretical framework (see figure 2.1) pos-its that religion and gender mold the women's political principles and the organizational pressures they face. These principles and pressures in turn combine with the political contexts in which the women live and work to shape the women's political priorities, their issue agendas, and their political strategies. These influences converge to empower many clergywomen to put the social justice mission into action in their own communities—but these influences also work in more complex and subtle ways to shape their choices concerning how to put faith into po-litical action.

Our guiding framework emphasizes that women clergy's own religious and political principles—which they bring with them to the ministry and rabbinate, and which often are reinforced by their experiences within this profession—have profound effects on the ways in which they approach politics. Much of the existing literature on political mobilization largely ignores the important role of normative incentives, which we call principles.[4] When scholars do discuss normative incentives, they are most likely to do so in post hoc explanations of activism levels that go above and beyond what would be explained by rational calculations of costs and benefits.[5] The fact that principles can help mobilize clergywomen, however, should not come as a surprise. Their very profession puts them in the business of encouraging others to live according to principles. Previous studies of clergy and politics have incorporated attention to religiously inspired political norms primarily through a focus on the key role that "social theology," which amounts to religiopolitical ideology, plays in shaping clergy's political choices.[6] This concept exemplifies one manifestation of the influence of principles that we have stressed throughout this book. Mainline Protestant and Jewish clergy tend to embrace similar progressive social theologies, which helps to explain their laserlike focus on justice and discrimination. Another key principle that runs through mainline Protestantism and Judaism is the imperative of providing guidance—and acknowledging a diversity of viewpoints—rather than merely telling people what to think.[7] We see profound evidence of the impact of this principle throughout our examinations of clergywomen's political choices. These two key principles (focusing on justice and providing guidance) exist in tension for many women, while other women gravitate toward one principle or the other. The first pushes women toward prophetic politics, whereas the second pulls them away from political action that might endanger their pastoral obligation to protect ministerial relationships.[8]

While much of this book confirms and expands what we already know about the religiopolitical values of mainline Protestant and Jewish clergy, our analysis of the importance of principles for women clergy brings to light two other key insights. The social justice focus is, for a good number of these women, infused with feminist ideology. This combination creates a strong commitment to a vision of justice that stresses

inclusiveness and the protection of rights, which is reflected in turn in
women clergy's political priorities and actions. We have also seen a
strong current of principles that are grounded in personal religious experiences. Many of the women feel directly called to act or to speak about
politics, and many indicate that their own personal theology encourages
their political action. Moreover, those women whose personal theology
encourages political action stand out as much more likely to give political
cues and engage in advocacy.

Our framework stresses that principles must compete with *pressures*
exerted upon women clergy by the religious organizations in which they
serve. The political culture of the United States emphasizes church-state
separation, and certain modes of political activism are widely seen as
unacceptable by religious leaders, laity, and constitutional scholars alike.
Moreover, each denomination and congregation has its own self-interest
to protect, which means that clergy are sometimes discouraged from
pursuing political activism, especially surrounding certain controversial
issues. These familiar strains are commonly sounded in research on
clergy activism.[9] Yet mainline Protestantism and Judaism still do create
religiopolitical contexts that seem to spur some clergywomen to pursue
political action, even to address the controversial and potentially divisive issues about which they personally care. In our examinations of both
the substantive and strategic nature of women clergy's political actions,
we find that organizational pressure plays a much smaller demobilizing
role than we had expected. At the same time, it is important to recall that
we focus only on low-level political mobilization—clergywomen undertaking *one* action out of a plethora of available options. Just because
many clergywomen manage to take one political action—even when
aimed at controversial issues—does not mean that we should conclude
that women clergy across the United States constitute a politicized feminist vanguard on the move. Moreover, evidence of widespread low-level
mobilization in no way reduces concerns about the need for stronger
moral political leadership from clergy and religious leaders. The reality
of the matter is that although many clergywomen display substantial political interest and awareness, there are clear limits to their willingness to
take political action. There is still latent political interest yet untapped—
and political injustices yet to be tackled.

At the congregational level, where one would expect the greatest evidence of clergy-laity gap–related demobilization, other stories emerge as far more noteworthy. Much has been made of the political constraints that conservative congregations can place on liberal clergy, and our results show that presiding over a conservative congregation does appear to restrict clergywomen's usage of some direct-action strategies. Our interviews and statistical analysis both point to the fact that congregational political *diversity* actually may be a more powerful constraint than congregational conservatism. Many women clergy subscribe to the view that one must first do no harm to one's congregation, a view that may be enhanced by gender socialization toward conflict avoidance. Political discussions bring out divisions, which lead to conflict and thus to concerns about alienating members who need pastoral care.

Positive stories about congregational mobilization also emerge throughout the book. Many individual congregations bring strong expectations of political action on the part of their clergy. This mobilization comes from congregations with strong histories of involvement; from those with memberships that include politically mobilized subgroups; or, consistent with our earlier findings, from congregations located in areas facing pressing public problems.[10] We find that such congregational expectations distinguish between clergywomen who engage in more controversial political activities and those who avoid such involvement.

Much of the extant literature on women clergy focuses on the professional discrimination and disadvantages that they face, which is relevant to our concept of organizational pressure.[11] Although we found much less explicit gender-oriented pressures against political action than we expected, clergywomen do acknowledge that they encounter various demobilizing pressures in the course of their everyday work. Some of these pressures (such as the time constraints of the job and the need to maintain ministerial relationships) are general in nature and would be expected to affect men equally. Other sorts of pressures, however, have a stronger gender basis. Among these would be added time constraints that flow either from family expectations or from a sense that women must be "twice as good as men." These findings highlight the importance of studying organizational *demobilization* as well as organizational mobilization.

Because much previous research on political activism among clergy stresses general political tasks (protesting, contacting officials, or campaigning) or activism in parachurch organizations (such as Christian Coalition) or secular organizations (such as Planned Parenthood), it was surprising to see how much the clergywomen do political work *within* their denominational bodies. Despite the trends cited by scholars that parachurch organizations are likely to eclipse the work of denominational groups, we find that denominational activism appears alive and well for clergywomen.[12] The evident relevance of denominational political outlets may mark a sort of religious institutionalization of political action. Little scholarly attention has been given to this phenomenon.[13] This advocacy activity has the advantage of organizational backing, because clergy are likely to be recruited and encouraged within their denominations to serve in such capacities. It has the added advantage of quelling (at least some) fears that stem from congregational pressures. Thus clergywomen can avail themselves of opportunities for political action despite gender-based challenges and enormous time pressures.

Another theme that comes across throughout the foregoing analyses is how women clergy's political priorities are shaped by local political context (but not by the national political agenda). Our interviews repeatedly produce evidence that clergywomen's political priorities often flow from specific local problems. Clergy frequently discuss the way that local problems lead them toward particular political issues or modes of political action. The old adage that all politics is local emerges as well in the fact that clergywomen did not appear to be more politically active during a presidential election year.

We also see the powerful influence of political recruitment upon mobilization. Women clergy frequently work with organizations that actively recruit them, such as Habitat for Humanity, Industrial Areas Foundation coalitions, and community-development and social service boards. Pro-choice organizations, civil libertarian groups, and other liberal interest groups—particularly those that deal with issues directly affecting women and children—might benefit from concerted efforts to *recruit* women clergy, as these women seem willing and able to express their advocacy for such issues if the conditions are right.

Future Research Directions

Research on women clergy is crucial, especially as their ranks continue to increase. In addition to the rapidly growing numbers of clergywomen in mainline Protestantism and Judaism, women are slowly advancing to positions of religious leadership within evangelical, Pentecostal, and African American Protestantism. The experiences these women have as religious leaders are doubtless different, at least in some ways, from those of the mainline Protestant and Jewish clergywomen we have analyzed here. Further research on such religious leaders is necessary.[14] Some scholars also predict that the Roman Catholic Church will begin ordaining women in the next century.[15] If this comes to pass, extensive research will be necessary to chart the incorporation of women into the priesthood.

Generally speaking, as the ministry and rabbinate incorporate more women, the political interests and actions of clergywomen will be all the more important to track. Moreover, our research shows that women clergy approach politics from a relatively consistent and distinctive vantage point, which is consistent with the widespread political gender gap that characterizes American politics today.[16] And their evident interest in and knowledge of politics suggests that, if anything, women clergy are likely to exert even more political clout in decades to come.

This book also highlights the vast range of political activities in which clergy engage, many of which are missed by standard survey questions. The enormous variety of clergywomen's political activities reveals how they adapt to the personal, organizational, and political constraints that they face every day. They seek out and utilize political strategies that work.

Our in-depth interviews uncover the rich and complex ways in which clergywomen's own principles intersect with both the pressures they face on the job and contemporary political circumstances to mold their political choices. The depth offered by these intensive interviews complements the breadth offered by the national survey data. Qualitative research helps us to refine the questions that we should ask when doing quantitative research, and it also helps us to uncover political phenomena

—especially related to the role of local context—that national surveys would have missed. Quantitative research, on the other hand, allows us to draw broad conclusions about clergywomen and their politics that would not have been possible on the basis of fifty-four interviews alone. Future research on clergy ought to embrace similar multi-method strategies so as to capture both the depth and breadth of clergy's political experiences. There is a particular need for additional multivariate analyses, like those we present in chapter 6, of the factors that contribute to the various dimensions of clergy's political choices.

We also set the stage for a normative debate about the appropriate political roles clergy should embrace. Most of the women who comment about teaching justice qualify their statements by explaining how crucial it is to teach people to listen to multiple sides of a debate so that they can reach their own conclusions. A Disciples of Christ minister exemplifies this position: "I always make sure that when I do [talk about politics], that I let people know how I got there, particularly around scripture, but making it very clear that there are other perspectives and insights." The roles clergy play in direct action are more complex. In some instances clergy may be acting in public witness on a social issue *qua clergy*. For example, they may appear at a protest or rally wearing a clerical collar, or they may list their names on a petition or advertisement with the title "Reverend" or "Rabbi" attached. In many instances clergy are recruited for direct action in their communities specifically for their moral legitimacy, occupational skills, or organizational resources. As a Presbyterian woman noted, "I think people often invite me to come and speak at a rally or come walk with them behind a banner *because* I am a woman clergy. And not just because I am a clergy, but because I am a *woman* clergy." In other cases, clergy may be acting more as ordinary citizens when they sign petitions, participate in boycotts, protest, or campaign without making reference to any clerical titles or resources. However, the delicate balance between clergy acting as moral leaders and clergy acting as citizens is not an easy or clear one. One woman explained, "I think twice about what I do since it is not just my own name but the congregation that follows me as well." These complexities highlight some of the challenges facing religious leaders as they work to develop shared understandings of clergy's appropriate political roles, as well as the challenges facing individual clergy as they struggle to develop principles to guide their own political actions.

Since this book focuses on clergywomen's experiences alone, our analysis of gender's political significance is limited to what women tell us about how they think gender affects their political choices. Future research, which we have already begun,[17] should focus on how the political views and actions of women pastors and rabbis differ from those of their male counterparts. Particularly useful would be further examinations of the role of the political dimensions of religious callings and how clergy's personal theological orientations affect their political choices. Are male clergy any more or less likely than their female counterparts to translate religious callings into political activity? Most central to future study of the role of gender in religious (and political) institutions is analysis of whether men and women respond differently to organizational pressures and politics. Are men less susceptible to organizational pressure than women? How do men and women differ in terms of recruitment into political opportunities?

More broadly, this study highlights the importance of investigating how people's professional lives affect their political lives.[18] Clergy are by no means the only citizens whose profession influences their political choices. Many issues remain to be explored concerning the political socialization and the political mobilization (and demobilization) of citizens via their workplace experiences. This emphasis echoes philosophers' and social scientists' longstanding interest in the political implications of the workplace.[19] Much of this work has focused on how the workplace influences the level or quality of political participation by workers. Our mobilization framework directs attention to a much broader array of questions concerning the intersection of the politics of work and the work of politics.

Clergywomen's Future Political World

Some scholars, most notably James Davison Hunter and Kimon Howland Sargeant, have argued that as more women enter the ministry, the religious traditions that ordain them will be socially and politically liberalized.[20] Indeed, women clergy's liberal political outlook, which we have documented in this book, means that their politics is perfectly in tune with the leaders of mainline Protestantism and Reform and Conservative Judaism, who have been liberal for generations as well. With the rise of Charitable Choice and faith-based initiatives, the antipoverty work that liberal clergywomen undertake, particularly in urban settings, could give new life to the recently invisible religious left.

However, liberalism on the part of clergy (both male and female) and their religious traditions could serve as a detriment if such political views rob them of their professional legitimacy. The much-documented clergy-laity gap plagues many mainline Protestant congregations.[21] Mainline Protestants whose political views clash with those of their clergy often exercise their right to religious freedom by selecting another alternative in the competitive American religious marketplace.[22] Jewish congregations also have a history of rejecting rabbis with whom they disagree politically.[23]

On the other hand, institutions change incrementally, and both mainline Protestantism and Judaism are certain to adapt and grow around the fact that so many of their current and future leaders are female. Despite some numeric decline, both traditions remain vital, energetic religious movements with plenty of devoted adherents.[24] The women whom these religious traditions will ordain in generations to come are also likely to differ from their pioneering predecessors in many ways. Above all, as more women enter the ministry and rabbinate, problems associated with gender-based discrimination ought to diminish. In a few generations (and arguably even sooner) women will be less likely to perceive themselves as feminist renegades—or be perceived as such by others—when they choose to enter a seminary or rabbinical school. Already roughly one-third of all American seminarians are female, so the stigma of outsider status has begun to diminish for women who aspire to be clergy. If women are no longer forced to battle every day for equality and acceptance, their political outlooks will probably diversify.

Today feminist socialization seems to provide a powerful rationale for some clergywomen to engage in political action. Likewise, their socialization experiences as a professional minority give them a unique vantage point from which to approach the political side of discrimination. The passion and conviction with which these women view such issues make them a valuable resource for political groups that champion progressive causes. Of course it is important to remember that, even today, not all clergywomen are lockstep liberals. For some, the experience of being a female religious leader does not result in an automatically left-leaning, feminist political perspective. Other clergywomen simply lack interest in politics in the first place.

Clergywomen have the potential to set political agendas for their congregations and possibly to influence the broader agendas of their religious traditions. Women clergy are uniquely situated as female—and in many instances feminist—voices in social institutions (religious congregations) that are designed explicitly to provide moral guidance. As such, they may be able to act as agenda setters not only for their congregations and denominations, but also beyond.

Notes

Chapter 1

1. In these profiles we use fictitious names and disguise city references in order to conceal the identity of study participants.

2. For wonderful accounts of the roles played by women, beginning with Hutchinson, through the history of American religion, see Rosemary Skinner Keller and Rosemary Radford Ruether, eds., *Women and Religion in America* (San Francisco: Harper and Row, 1981), and Rosemary Skinner Keller and Rosemary Radford Ruether, eds., *In Our Own Voices: Four Centuries of American Women's Religious Writing* (Louisville: Westminster John Knox, 1995).

3. The *Declaration of Sentiments and Resolutions* was a bold assertion of women's equality modeled after the Declaration of Independence. See Elizabeth Cady Stanton, Susan B. Anthony, and Matilda Joslyn Gage, eds., *History of Woman Suffrage*, Vol. 1 (Rochester: Charles Mann, 1881), 73.

4. Frances E. Willard, *Woman in the Pulpit* (Chicago: Woman's Christian Temperance Publication Association, 1889).

5. For a historical look at the roles played by nuns, see Carol K. Coburn and Martha Smith, *Spirited Lives: How Nuns Shaped Catholic Culture and American Life, 1836–1920* (Chapel Hill: University of North Carolina Press, 1999); for a more recent look, see Lucy Kaylin, *For the Love of God: The Faith and Future of the American Nun* (New York: William Morrow, 2000), and Lora Ann Quiñonez and Mary Daniel Turner, *The Transformation of American Catholic Sisters* (Philadelphia: Temple University Press, 1992).

6. Robert Booth Fowler, Allen D. Hertzke, and Laura R. Olson, *Religion and Politics in America: Faith, Culture, and Strategic Choices*, 2nd ed. (Boulder: Westview, 1999), chapter 8; Robert Wuthnow, *The Restructuring of American Re-*

ligion: Society and Faith since World War II (Princeton: Princeton University Press, 1988), 225–26.

7. Mark Chaves, *Ordaining Women: Culture and Conflict in Religious Organizations* (Cambridge, MA: Harvard University Press, 1997), notes that 1 Corinthians 14:33–35 is also used to argue against women's ordination.

8. Chaves, *Ordaining Women,* also points to 1 Corinthians 11:4–5 and Acts 2:16–18 as scriptural support of women in ministry.

9. Edward C. Lehman, *Women Clergy: Breaking through Gender Barriers* (New Brunswick: Transaction, 1985); Wuthnow, *Restructuring.*

10. Patricia M. Y. Chang, "Female Clergy in the Contemporary Protestant Church: A Current Assessment," *Journal for the Scientific Study of Religion* 36 (1997): 565–73; Barbara Brown Zikmund, Adair T. Lummis, and Patricia Mei Yin Chang, *Clergy Women: An Uphill Calling* (Louisville: Westminster John Knox, 1998). This story has also been covered in the press. See especially Jennifer Gonzalez, "Hitting the Stained Glass Ceiling," *The Cleveland Plain Dealer,* 12 December 1998, 1F; Gustav Niebuhr, "Following Mothers, Women Heed Call to Nation's Pulpits," *The New York Times,* 25 April 1999, A1.

11. Karen M. Kaufmann and John R. Petrocik, "The Changing Politics of American Men: Understanding the Sources of the Gender Gap," *American Journal of Political Science* 43 (1999): 864–87; Margaret C. Trevor, "Political Socialization, Party Identification, and the Gender Gap," *Public Opinion Quarterly* 63 (1999): 62–78; Susan Welch, "Women as Political Animals? A Test of Some Explanations for Male-Female Political Participation Differences," *American Journal of Political Science* 21 (1977): 711–30.

12. James L. Guth, John C. Green, Corwin E. Smidt, and Lyman A. Kellstedt, "Women Clergy and the Political Transformation of Mainline Protestantism," presented at the annual meeting of the Social Science History Association, Atlanta, 1994; Zikmund, Lummis, and Chang, 18–22.

13. James Davison Hunter and Kimon Howland Sargeant, "Religion and the Transformation of Public Culture," *Social Research* 60 (1993): 545–70. On the general notion of "culture wars," see James Davison Hunter, *Culture Wars: The Struggle to Define America* (New York: Basic Books, 1991), and James Davison Hunter, *Before the Shooting Begins: Searching for Democracy in America's Culture War* (New York: Free Press, 1994).

14. See, for example, Jackson W. Carroll, Barbara Hargrove, and Adair T. Lummis, *Women of the Cloth: A New Opportunity for the Churches* (San Francisco: Harper and Row, 1983); Chaves, *Ordaining Women;* Barbara Finlay, "Do Men and Women Have Different Goals for Ministry? Evidence from Seminarians," *Sociology of Religion* 57 (1996): 311–18; Lehman; Paula Nesbitt, "Clergy Femini-

zation: Controlled Labor or Transformative Change?" *Journal for the Scientific Study of Religion* 36 (1997): 585–98; Zikmund, Lummis, and Chang.

15. E. Wilbur Bock, "The Female Clergy: A Case of Professional Marginality," *American Journal of Sociology* 72 (1967): 531–39; Carroll, Hargrove, and Lummis; Finlay; Martha Long Ice, *Clergy Women and Their Worldviews: Calling for a New Age* (Westport: Praeger, 1987); Lehman; Nesbitt; Frederick W. Schmidt, *A Still Small Voice: Women, Ordination, and the Church* (Syracuse: Syracuse University Press, 1996); Zikmund, Lummis, and Chang.

16. Joy Charlton, "What It Means to Go First: Clergywomen of the Pioneer Generation," presented at the annual meeting of the Society for the Scientific Study of Religion, St. Louis, 1995; Virginia Culver, "Methodists See More Female Clergy Depart," *The Denver Post*, 26 February 1999, B5.

17. Among the best historical sources on women's ordination are Chaves, *Ordaining Women;* Carl J. Schneider and Dorothy Schneider, *In Their Own Right: The History of American Clergywomen* (New York: Crossroad, 1997); Barbara Brown Zikmund, "Women and Ordination," in Keller and Ruether, eds., *In Our Own Voices.*

18. Chaves, *Ordaining Women,* 16; Zikmund, 296; Zikmund, Lummis, and Chang, 9.

19. See Nancy McGlen, Karen O'Connor, Laura van Assendelft, and Wendy Gunther-Canada, *Women, Politics, and American Society,* 3rd ed. (New York: Longman, 2002), 5–6.

20. Ibid., 1.

21. Janet Zollinger Giele, *Two Paths to Women's Equality: Temperance, Suffrage, and the Origins of Modern Feminism* (Old Tappan, NJ: Twayne, 1995).

22. We use dates reported by Zikmund, but Chaves, *Ordaining Women,* offers different dates for the AME Church (1960) and the CME Church (1966). The difference would seem to lie in the time lapsed between formal denominational policy change and the actual ordination of the first woman.

23. Mary Daly, *The Church and the Second Sex* (New York: Harper and Row, 1968); Betty Friedan, *The Feminine Mystique* (New York: Dell, 1963).

24. Chaves, *Ordaining Women,* 19–20.

25. For information on the history of women's ordination, see Chaves, *Ordaining Women,* chapter 2; Zikmund; Zikmund, Lummis, and Chang, 7–12.

26. Christel Manning, *God Gave Us the Right: Conservative Catholic, Evangelical Protestant, and Orthodox Jewish Women Grapple with Feminism* (New Brunswick: Rutgers University Press, 1999); John Paul II, *Ordinatio Sacerdotalis: Apostolic Letter on Reserving Priestly Ordination to Men Alone* (Boston: Pauline Books, 1994).

27. For a broader discussion of feminist dissent within the Catholic Church, see Mary Fainsod Katzenstein, *Faithful and Fearless: Moving Feminist Protest inside the Church and Military* (Princeton: Princeton University Press, 1998). On the priest shortage in the United States, see Richard A. Schoenherr and Lawrence A. Young, *Full Pews and Empty Altars: Demographics of the Priest Shortage in United States Catholic Dioceses* (Madison: University of Wisconsin Press, 1993), and Richard A. Schoenherr, *Goodbye Father: The Celibate Male Priesthood and the Future of the Catholic Church* (New York: Oxford University Press, 2002).

28. Manning, 105.

29. Chaves, *Ordaining Women;* Michael Lienesch, *Redeeming America: Piety and Politics in the New Christian Right* (Chapel Hill: University of North Carolina Press, 1993); Manning.

30. For a discussion of Pentecostal and African American women clergy, see Charles H. Barfoot and Gerald T. Sheppard, "Prophetic vs. Priestly Religion: The Changing Role of Women Clergy in Classical Pentecostal Churches," *Review of Religious Research* 22 (1980): 2–17; Cheryl Townsend Gilkes, "Together and in Harness: Women's Traditions in the Sanctified Church," in Micheline R. Malson, Elisabeth Mudimbe-Boyi, Jean F. O'Barr, and Mary Wyer, eds., *Black Women in America: Social Science Perspectives* (Chicago: University of Chicago Press, 1990); Elaine J. Lawless, *Handmaidens of the Lord: Pentecostal Women Preachers and Traditional Religion* (Philadelphia: University of Pennsylvania Press, 1988); and Cheryl J. Sanders, "History of Women in the Pentecostal Movement," *Cyberjournal for Pentecostal-Charismatic Research* 2 (1997): 1–13.

31. "Southern Baptist Convention Passes Resolution Opposing Women as Pastors," *The New York Times,* 15 June 2000, A18.

32. Jimmy Carter was quoted in "Perspectives," *Newsweek,* 30 October 2000, 31.

33. Kaufmann and Petrocik; Trevor; Welch.

34. See Nancy Burns, Kay Lehman Schlozman, and Sidney Verba, *The Private Roots of Public Action: Gender, Equality, and Political Participation* (Cambridge, MA: Harvard University Press, 2001), 32, although they note that race and class are likely to create bigger voting cleavages in American politics.

35. Virginia Sapiro, *The Political Integration of Women: Roles, Socialization, and Politics* (Urbana: University of Illinois Press, 1983). See also Kristi Andersen, "Working Women and Political Participation, 1952–1972," *American Journal of Political Science* 19 (1975): 439–55; Susan Bourque and Jean Grossholtz, "Politics as an Unnatural Practice: Political Science Looks at Female Participation," *Poli-*

tics and Society 4 (1974): 255–66; Cal Clark and Janet Clark, "Models of Gender and Political Participation in the United States," *Women and Politics* 6 (1986): 5–25; Maurice Duverger, *The Political Role of Women* (New York: UNESCO, 1955); Nancy McGlen, "The Impact of Parenthood on Political Participation," *Western Political Quarterly* 33 (1980): 297–313; Kay Lehman Schlozman, Nancy Burns, and Sidney Verba, "Gender and the Pathways to Participation: The Role of Resources," *Journal of Politics* 56 (1994): 963–90; Kay Lehman Schlozman, Nancy Burns, and Sidney Verba, "'What Happened at Work Today?' A Multi-stage Model of Gender, Employment, and Political Participation," *Journal of Politics* 61 (1999): 29–53; Welch.

36. See Burns, Schlozman, and Verba.

37. Schlozman, Burns, and Verba, "'What Happened at Work?'"

38. On women as government elites, see Clara Bingham, *Women on the Hill: Challenging the Culture of Congress* (New York: Times Books, 1997); Kim Fridkin Kahn, *The Political Consequences of Being a Woman: How Stereotypes Influence the Conduct and Consequences of Political Campaigns* (New York: Columbia University Press, 1996); Lyn Kathlene, "Power and Influence in State Legislative Policy Making: The Interaction of Gender and Position in Committee Hearing Debates," *American Political Science Review* 43 (1994): 864–87; and Barbara Norrander and Clyde Wilcox, "The Geography of Gender Power: Women in State Legislatures," in Sue Thomas and Clyde Wilcox, eds., *Women and Elective Office: Past, Present, and Future* (New York: Oxford University Press, 1998). On women as business elites, see Rosabeth Moss Kanter, *Men and Women of the Corporation,* 2nd ed. (New York: Basic Books, 1993), and Suzanne Uttaro Samuels, *Fetal Rights, Women's Rights: Gender Equality in the Workplace* (Madison: University of Wisconsin Press, 1995). On women in the military, see Judith Hicks Stiehm, *Arms and the Enlisted Woman* (Philadelphia: Temple University Press, 1989).

39. Charitable Choice allows states to provide federal funding to religious congregations for social services. See Pub. L. 104–93, 22 August 1996, The Personal Responsibility and Work Opportunity Reconciliation Act of 1996, Section 104. For a discussion of the willingness of congregations to take advantage of Charitable Choice funding, see Mark Chaves, "Religious Congregations and Welfare Reform: Who Will Take Advantage of 'Charitable Choice'?" *American Sociological Review* 64 (1999): 836–46. For an example of the efforts of a local government to partner with congregations, see the discussion of Indianapolis in Sue E. S. Crawford, "Clergy at Work in the Secular City," (Ph.D. diss., Indiana University, 1995).

40. Fowler, Hertzke, and Olson.

41. C. Kirk Hadaway, Penny Long Marler, and Mark Chaves, "What the Polls Don't Show: A Closer Look at U.S. Church Attendance," *American Sociological Review* 58 (1993): 741–52.

42. Laura R. Olson, *Filled with Spirit and Power: Protestant Clergy in Politics* (Albany: State University of New York Press, 2000).

43. James C. Cavendish, "To March or Not to March: Clergy Mobilization Strategies and Grassroots Antidrug Activism," in Sue E. S. Crawford and Laura R. Olson, eds., *Christian Clergy in American Politics* (Baltimore: Johns Hopkins University Press, 2001); Christopher P. Gilbert, *The Impact of Churches on Political Behavior: An Empirical Study* (Westport: Greenwood Press, 1993); Kenneth D. Wald, Dennis E. Owen, and Samuel S. Hill, "Churches as Political Communities," *American Political Science Review* 82 (1988): 531–48; Kenneth D. Wald, Dennis E. Owen, and Samuel S. Hill, "Political Cohesion in Churches," *Journal of Politics* 52 (1990): 197–215.

44. Crawford; James L. Guth, John C. Green, Corwin E. Smidt, Lyman A. Kellstedt, and Margaret M. Poloma, *The Bully Pulpit: The Politics of Protestant Clergy* (Lawrence, KS: University Press of Kansas, 1997); Ted G. Jelen, *The Political World of the Clergy* (Westport: Praeger, 1993); Olson, *Filled with Spirit*.

45. For clergy participation in policy discussions, see Crawford. For clergy involvement in coalitions on poverty and violence, see Olson, *Filled with Spirit*. On the relationship between clergy and the civil rights movement, see Aldon D. Morris, *The Origins of the Civil Rights Movement: Black Communities Organizing for Change* (New York: Free Press, 1984).

46. See Ted G. Jelen, "Notes for a Theory of Clergy as Political Leaders," in Crawford and Olson, eds., *Christian Clergy*.

47. Ernest Q. Campbell and Thomas F. Pettigrew, *Christians in Racial Crisis: A Study of Little Rock's Ministry* (Washington, DC: Public Affairs Press, 1959); Jeffrey K. Hadden, *The Gathering Storm in the Churches* (Garden City, NY: Doubleday, 1969); Harold E. Quinley, *The Prophetic Clergy: Social Activism among Protestant Ministers* (New York: Wiley, 1974); Rodney Stark, Bruce D. Foster, Charles Y. Glock, and Harold E. Quinley, *Wayward Shepherds: Prejudice and the Protestant Clergy* (New York: Harper and Row, 1971).

48. Paul A. Djupe and Christopher P. Gilbert, *The Prophetic Pulpit: Clergy, Churches, and Communities in American Politics* (Lanham, MD: Rowman and Littlefield, 2003); Guth et al., *Bully Pulpit*; Jelen, *Political World*; Olson, *Filled with Spirit*.

49. H. Richard Niebuhr, *Christ and Culture* (New York: Harper and Row, 1951). See also David A. Roozen, William McKinney, and Jackson W. Carroll, *Varieties of Religious Presence: Mission in Public Life* (New York: Pilgrim Press,

1984); Robert Wuthnow, *Acts of Compassion: Caring for Others and Helping Ourselves* (Princeton: Princeton University Press, 1991).

50. See Fowler, Hertzke, and Olson.

Chapter 2

1. See, for example, David Easton, *A Systems Analysis of Political Life* (Chicago: University of Chicago Press, 1979).

2. For an overview of work on political participation, see M. Margaret Conway, *Political Participation in the United States,* 2nd ed. (Washington, DC: CQ Press, 1991); Steven J. Rosenstone and John Mark Hansen, *Mobilization, Participation, and Democracy* (New York: Macmillan, 1993); and Sidney Verba, Kay Lehman Schlozman, and Henry E. Brady, *Voice and Equality: Civic Voluntarism in American Politics* (Cambridge, MA: Harvard University Press, 1995).

3. Ram A. Cnaan, *The Invisible Caring Hand: American Congregations and the Provision of Welfare* (New York: New York University Press, 2002); Ram A. Cnaan, *The Newer Deal: Social Work and Religion in Partnership* (New York: Columbia University Press, 1999); E. J. Dionne and Ming Hsu Chen, eds., *Sacred Places, Civic Purposes: Should Government Help Faith-based Charity?* (Washington, DC: The Brookings Institution, 2001).

4. See also Verba, Schlozman, and Brady, who employ broad definitions of the political, as well as our work on this matter in Sue E. S. Crawford, Laura R. Olson, and Melissa M. Deckman, "Understanding the Mobilization of Professionals," *Nonprofit and Voluntary Sector Quarterly* 30 (2001): 321–50. In general, studies of faith-based initiatives broaden definitions of the political while also moving studies of religiopolitical activism (in particular) well into the mainstream of political science.

5. The Presbyterian office in Washington, D.C., did not provide a list of women clergy. The list of Washington Presbyterian women was compiled instead via the Yellow Pages. This means that some of the smaller Presbyterian churches, which might not have placed an advertisement that named their ministers in the Yellow Pages, may not have been included in the list from which the sample was drawn.

6. Out of sixty-two women contacted to take part in this study, fifty-four (or 87 percent) agreed to participate, with rates of participation ranging from 73 to 100 percent in the four cities.

7. Sherrie Steiner and Donald Gray of Eastern College undertook the survey of American Baptist clergy. The authors of this book undertook the survey of Disciples of Christ clergy. Daniel Hofrenning of St. Olaf College undertook the survey of Evangelical Lutheran Church in America clergy. Paul Djupe of

Denison University undertook the survey of Jewish rabbis. Beau Weston of Centre College undertook the survey of Presbyterian Church (U.S.A.) clergy. John Green of the University of Akron undertook the survey of United Methodist clergy.

8. On this point see Charles H. Barfoot and Gerald T. Sheppard, "Prophetic vs. Priestly Religion: The Changing Role of Women Clergy in Classical Pentecostal Churches," *Review of Religious Research* 22 (1980): 2–17; Cheryl Townsend Gilkes, "Together and in Harness: Women's Traditions in the Sanctified Church," in Micheline R. Malson, Elisabeth Mudimbe-Boyi, Jean F. O'Barr, and Mary Wyer, eds., *Black Women in America: Social Science Perspectives* (Chicago: University of Chicago Press, 1990); Elaine J. Lawless, *Handmaidens of the Lord: Pentecostal Women Preachers and Traditional Religion* (Philadelphia: University of Pennsylvania Press, 1988); and Cheryl J. Sanders, "History of Women in the Pentecostal Movement," *Cyberjournal for Pentecostal-Charismatic Research* 2 (1997): 1–13.

9. Two traditions with large proportions of women ministers—the Unitarian Universalist Association and the Quakers (Friends)—could not be included in our study because the number of women ministers per city would have been so small.

10. Robert Booth Fowler, Allen D. Hertzke, and Laura R. Olson, *Religion and Politics in America: Faith, Culture, and Strategic Choices*, 2nd ed. (Boulder: Westview, 1999); Andrew Kohut, John C. Green, Scott Keeter, and Robert C. Toth, *The Diminishing Divide: Religion's Changing Role in American Politics* (Washington, DC: The Brookings Institution, 2000).

11. Kohut et al.; Robert Wuthnow, "Beyond Quiet Influence? Possibilities for the Protestant Mainline," in Robert Wuthnow and John H. Evans, eds., *The Quiet Hand of God: Faith-Based Activism and the Public Role of Mainline Protestantism* (Berkeley: University of California Press, 2002); Robert Wuthnow, "The Moral Minority," *The American Prospect* 11 (22 May 2000).

12. Sue E. S. Crawford, "Clergy at Work in the Secular City," Ph.D. diss., Indiana University, 1995; Melissa M. Deckman, *School Board Battles: The Christian Right in Local Politics* (Washington, DC: Georgetown University Press, 2004); Laura R. Olson, *Filled with Spirit and Power: Protestant Clergy in Politics* (Albany: State University of New York Press, 2000).

13. Crawford, Olson, and Deckman.

14. Lesley Stevens, "Different Voice/Different Voices: Anglican Women in Ministry," *Review of Religious Research* 30 (1989): 262–75.

15. Melissa M. Deckman, Sue E. S. Crawford, Laura R. Olson, and John C.

Green, "Clergy and the Politics of Gender: Women and Political Opportunity in Mainline Protestant Churches," *Journal for the Scientific Study of Religion* 42 (2003): 621–32.

16. More broadly, James Guth and colleagues find that personal differences in socioeconomic status do not correlate with political differences among clergy. See James L. Guth, John C. Green, Corwin E. Smidt, Lyman A. Kellstedt, and Margaret M. Poloma, *The Bully Pulpit: The Politics of Protestant Clergy* (Lawrence, KS: University Press of Kansas, 1997).

17. Ibid., 12.

18. See, for example, Robert Huckfeldt and John Sprague, *Citizens, Politics, and Social Communication: Information and Influence in an Election Campaign* (New York: Cambridge University Press, 1995); Rosenstone and Hansen; and Verba, Schlozman, and Brady.

19. See Paul A. Djupe and Christopher P. Gilbert, *The Prophetic Pulpit: Clergy, Churches, and Communities in American Politics* (Lanham, MD: Rowman and Littlefield, 2003).

20. Guth et al., *Bully Pulpit*, 21, refer to this concept as an "issue agenda."

21. This framework is a simplified version of a larger general model of professional mobilization that we develop elsewhere. See Crawford, Olson, and Deckman.

22. Deckman et al., "Clergy and the Politics of Gender"; James L. Guth, John C. Green, Corwin E. Smidt, and Lyman A. Kellstedt, "Women Clergy and the Political Transformation of Mainline Protestantism," presented at the annual meeting of the Social Science History Association, Atlanta, 1994.

23. Barbara Brown Zikmund, Adair T. Lummis, and Patricia Mei Yin Chang, *Clergy Women: An Uphill Calling* (Louisville: Westminster John Knox, 1998).

24. Djupe and Gilbert; Guth et al., *Bully Pulpit*; Ted G. Jelen, *The Political World of the Clergy* (Westport: Praeger, 1993); Olson, *Filled with Spirit*.

25. Crawford; Guth et al., *Bully Pulpit*; Jelen, *Political World*; Olson, *Filled with Spirit*.

26. See Guth et al., *Bully Pulpit*.

27. On the "clergy-laity gap," which posits that mainline Protestant clergy are more liberal than most members of their congregations, see James L. Adams, *The Growing Church Lobby in Washington* (Grand Rapids: Eerdmans, 1970); Jeffrey K. Hadden, *The Gathering Storm in the Churches* (Garden City, NY: Doubleday, 1969); and Norman B. Koller and Joseph D. Retzer, "The Sounds of Silence Revisited," *Sociological Analysis* 41 (1980): 155–61.

28. Crawford; Sue E. S. Crawford, Melissa M. Deckman, and Christi J. Braun, "Gender and the Political Choices of Women Clergy," in Sue E. S. Crawford and Laura R. Olson, eds., *Christian Clergy in American Politics* (Baltimore: Johns Hopkins University Press, 2001); Sue E. S. Crawford and Laura R. Olson, "Clergy as Political Actors in Urban Contexts," in Crawford and Olson, eds., *Christian Clergy;* Olson, *Filled with Spirit;* Laura R. Olson, "Mainline Protestant Washington Offices and the Political Lives of Clergy," in Wuthnow and Evans, eds., *Quiet Hand of God.*

29. For an extended discussion of the rational incentive for congregations to work locally, see Olson, "Mainline Protestant Washington Offices."

30. Crawford.

31. Previous studies have made arguments and presented data that led us to this expectation. See Rita Mae Kelly, "Offensive Men, Defensive Women: Sexual Harassment, Leadership, and Management," in Georgia Duerst-Lahti and Rita Mae Kelly, eds., *Gender Power, Leadership, and Governance* (Ann Arbor: University of Michigan Press, 1995); Frederick W. Schmidt, *A Still Small Voice: Women, Ordination, and the Church* (Syracuse: Syracuse University Press, 1996); Roberta S. Sigel, *Ambition and Accommodation: How Women View Gender Relations* (Chicago: University of Chicago Press, 1996).

32. E. Wilbur Bock, "The Female Clergy: A Case of Professional Marginality," *American Journal of Sociology* 72 (1967): 531–39; Martha Long Ice, *Clergy Women and Their Worldviews: Calling for a New Age* (Westport: Praeger, 1987); Olson, *Filled with Spirit;* Schmidt.

33. Verba, Schlozman, and Brady.

34. See Mark Chaves, "Religious Congregations and Welfare Reform: Who Will Take Advantage of 'Charitable Choice'?" *American Sociological Review* 64 (1999): 836–46; Cnaan, *Invisible Caring Hand;* Cnaan, *Newer Deal.*

Chapter 3

1. Émile Durkheim, *The Elementary Forms of the Religious Life* (1912; reprint, New York: Free Press, 1995), 44.

2. Ibid., 38.

3. H. Richard Niebuhr, *Christ and Culture* (New York: Harper and Row, 1951). See also David A. Roozen, William McKinney, and Jackson W. Carroll, *Varieties of Religious Presence: Mission in Public Life* (New York: Pilgrim Press, 1984), and Robert Wuthnow, *Acts of Compassion: Caring for Others and Helping Ourselves* (Princeton: Princeton University Press, 1991).

4. Here we must distinguish our use of the term *calling,* which implies an

invitation from God to enter the ministry, from another common usage that involves being invited to take a formal job with a congregation.

5. Larry Cochran, *The Sense of Vocation: A Study of Career and Life Develop-ment* (Albany: State University of New York Press, 1990). But see James L. Guth, "Reflections on the Status of Research on Clergy in Politics," in Sue E. S. Crawford and Laura R. Olson, eds., *Christian Clergy in American Politics* (Balti-more: Johns Hopkins University Press, 2001), for an example of a study that takes the concepts of socialization and career choice very seriously.

6. James L. Guth, John C. Green, Corwin E. Smidt, Lyman A. Kellstedt, and Margaret M. Poloma, *The Bully Pulpit: The Politics of Protestant Clergy* (Lawrence, KS: University Press of Kansas, 1997); Ted G. Jelen, *The Political World of the Clergy* (Westport: Praeger, 1993).

7. Interestingly, Barbara Brown Zikmund and her colleagues report that women clergy are more likely than their male counterparts to say that they entered the ministry due to a divine calling. See Barbara Brown Zikmund, Adair T. Lummis, and Patricia Mei Yin Chang, *Clergy Women: An Uphill Calling* (Louisville: Westminster John Knox, 1998), 94.

8. Marie T. Coombs and Francis K. Nemeck, *Called by God: A Theology of Vocation and Lifelong Commitment* (Collegeville, MN: Liturgical Press, 1992).

9. Adrienne Von Speyr, *They Followed His Call: Vocation and Asceticism* (New York: Alba House, 1995).

10. On the debates about homosexuality within mainline Protestantism, see Wendy Cadge, "Vital Conflicts: The Mainline Protestant Denominations De-bate Homosexuality," in Robert Wuthnow and John H. Evans, eds., *The Quiet Hand of God: Faith-Based Activism and the Public Role of Mainline Protestantism* (Berkeley: University of California Press, 2002).

11. Jelen, *Political World.*

12. Durkheim, 44; emphasis added.

13. Guth et al., *Bully Pulpit.*

14. Jackson W. Carroll, Barbara G. Wheeler, Daniel O. Aleshire, and Penny Long Marler, *Being There: Culture and Formation in Two Theological Schools* (New York: Oxford University Press, 1997); Guth.

15. Allen D. Hertzke, *Representing God in Washington: The Role of Religious Lobbies in the American Polity* (Knoxville: University of Tennessee Press, 1988); Daniel J. B. Hofrenning, *In Washington but Not of It: The Prophetic Politics of Re-ligious Lobbyists* (Philadelphia: Temple University Press, 1995); Laura R. Olson, "Mainline Protestant Washington Offices and the Political Lives of Clergy," in Wuthnow and Evans, eds., *Quiet Hand of God.*

16. Niebuhr, 86.

17. The United Methodist Church, *The Book of Discipline* 2000 (Nashville: Abingdon Press, 2000), par. 164B.

18. Charles S. Liebman and Steven M. Cohen, *Two Worlds of Judaism: The Israeli and American Experiences* (New Haven: Yale University Press, 1990).

19. Patricia M. Y. Chang, "Female Clergy in the Contemporary Protestant Church: A Current Assessment," *Journal for the Scientific Study of Religion* 36 (1997): 565–73; Edward C. Lehman, *Women Clergy: Breaking through Gender Barriers* (New Brunswick: Transaction, 1985).

20. Carroll et al., *Being There.*

21. Guth et al., *Bully Pulpit.*

22. This finding is consistent with the results reported by Olson, "Mainline Protestant Washington Offices."

23. Ibid.

24. Arlie Hochschild, *The Second Shift: Working Parents and the Revolution at Home* (New York: Viking Press, 1989).

25. Mark Chaves, *Ordaining Women: Culture and Conflict in Religious Organizations* (Cambridge, MA: Harvard University Press, 1997).

26. James R. Wood, *Leadership in Voluntary Organizations: The Controversy over Social Action in Protestant Churches* (New Brunswick: Rutgers University Press, 1981).

27. James Davison Hunter and Kimon Howland Sargeant, "Religion and the Transformation of Public Culture," *Social Research* 60 (1993): 545–70.

28. Lehman.

Chapter 4

1. Sidney Verba and Norman H. Nie, *Participation in America: Political Democracy and Social Equality* (Chicago: University of Chicago Press, 1972), 271.

2. Steven J. Rosenstone and John Mark Hansen, *Mobilization, Participation, and Democracy in America* (New York: Macmillan, 1993).

3. On the general notion of opinion leadership, see Elihu Katz and Paul F. Lazarsfeld, *Personal Influence: The Part Played by People in the Flow of Mass Communications* (New York: Free Press, 1955).

4. James L. Guth, John C. Green, Corwin E. Smidt, and Lyman A. Kellstedt, "Women Clergy and the Political Transformation of Mainline Protestantism," presented at the annual meeting of the Social Science History Association, Atlanta, 1994; James L. Guth, John C. Green, Corwin E. Smidt, Lyman A. Kellstedt, and Margaret M. Poloma, *The Bully Pulpit: The Politics of Protestant Clergy* (Lawrence, KS: University Press of Kansas, 1997).

5. Jackson W. Carroll, Barbara Hargrove, and Adair T. Lummis, *Women of the Cloth: A New Opportunity for the Churches* (San Francisco: Harper and Row, 1983).

6. Barbara Brown Zikmund, Adair T. Lummis, and Patricia Mei Yin Chang, *Clergy Women: An Uphill Calling* (Louisville: Westminster John Knox, 1998).

7. Jackson W. Carroll, Barbara G. Wheeler, Daniel O. Aleshire, and Penny Long Marler, *Being There: Culture and Formation in Two Theological Schools* (New York: Oxford University Press, 1997); see also Sandra Hughes Boyd, "A Woman's Journey toward Priesthood: An Autobiographical Study from the 1950s through the 1980s," in Catherine M. Prelinger, ed., *Episcopal Women: Gender, Spirituality, and Commitment in an American Mainline Denomination* (New York: Oxford University Press, 1992).

8. Harold Lasswell, *Politics: Who Gets What, When, How* (New York: World, 1958).

9. See Wendy Cadge, "Vital Conflicts: The Mainline Protestant Denominations Debate Homosexuality," in Robert Wuthnow and John H. Evans, eds., *The Quiet Hand of God: Faith-Based Activism and the Public Role of Mainline Protestantism* (Berkeley: University of California Press, 2002).

10. See Julia McCord, "Pastor's Trial May Be Crossroads for Church," *The Omaha World-Herald*, 8 March 1997, 1A.

11. See Sue E. S. Crawford, Melissa M. Deckman, and Christi J. Braun, "Gender and the Political Choices of Women Clergy," in Sue E. S. Crawford and Laura R. Olson, eds., *Christian Clergy in American Politics* (Baltimore: Johns Hopkins University Press, 2001); Laura R. Olson, *Filled with Spirit and Power: The Politics of Protestant Clergy* (Albany: State University of New York Press, 2000); Laura R. Olson, Sue E. S. Crawford, and James L. Guth, "Changing Issue Agendas of Women Clergy," *Journal for the Scientific Study of Religion* 39 (2000): 140–53.

12. Carroll et al., *Being There.*

13. Brian Steensland, "The Hydra and the Swords: Social Welfare and Mainline Advocacy, 1964–2000," in Wuthnow and Evans, eds., *Quiet Hand of God*; Bradford Verter, "Furthering the Freedom Struggle: Racial Justice Activism in the Churches since the Civil Rights Era," in Wuthnow and Evans, eds., *Quiet Hand of God.*

14. See Laura R. Olson, "Mainline Protestant Washington Offices and the Political Lives of Clergy," in Wuthnow and Evans, eds., *Quiet Hand of God.* For further theoretical discussion, see Roger Finke and Rodney Stark, *The Churching of America, 1776–1990: Winners and Losers in Our Religious Economy* (New Brunswick: Rutgers University Press, 1992), and James K. Wellman, *The*

Gold Coast Church and the Ghetto: Christ and Culture in Mainline Protestantism (Urbana: University of Illinois Press, 1999). For evidence that there is an incentive to embrace issues that are of interest to the local community, see Sue E. S. Crawford, "Clergy at Work in the Secular City," Ph.D. diss., Indiana University, 1995; Crawford, Deckman, and Braun; Sue E. S. Crawford and Laura R. Olson, "Clergy as Political Actors in Urban Contexts," in Crawford and Olson, eds., *Christian Clergy;* and Olson, *Filled with Spirit.*

15. See Crawford and Olson; Finke and Stark; Olson, *Filled with Spirit;* and Wellman.

16. See Olson, *Filled with Spirit,* for a wide-ranging discussion of this point.

17. John W. Kingdon, *Agendas, Alternatives, and Public Policies,* 2nd ed. (New York: Harper Collins, 1995), 3.

18. Shanto Iyengar and Donald R. Kinder, *News That Matters: Television and American Opinion* (Chicago: University of Chicago Press, 1987).

19. Gallup Organization, *Gallup Poll Trends: "Most Important Problem"* (1999), http://www.gallup.com/poll/trends/ptproblem.asp.

20. The women's concerns about poverty and hunger are not coded as economic issues in our urban interview sample; the economic issues on the public agenda largely involve taxation and business regulation.

21. E. Wilbur Bock, "The Female Clergy: A Case of Professional Marginality," *American Journal of Sociology* 72 (1967): 531–39; Carroll, Hargrove, and Lummis; Barbara Finlay, "Do Men and Women Have Different Goals for Ministry? Evidence from Seminarians," *Sociology of Religion* 57 (1996): 311–18; Martha Long Ice, *Clergy Women and Their Worldviews: Calling for a New Age* (Westport: Praeger, 1987); Edward C. Lehman, *Women Clergy: Breaking through Gender Barriers* (New Brunswick: Transaction, 1985); Paula Nesbitt, "Clergy Feminization: Controlled Labor or Transformative Change?" *Journal for the Scientific Study of Religion* 36 (1997): 585–98; Frederick W. Schmidt, *A Still Small Voice: Women, Ordination, and the Church* (Syracuse: Syracuse University Press, 1996).

22. Virginia Sapiro, *The Political Integration of Women: Roles, Socialization, and Politics* (Urbana: University of Illinois Press, 1983).

23. Sue E. S. Crawford and Kristin Kadleck, "The Workplace Experiences of Women Clergy: Does the Personal Become Political?" presented at the annual meeting of the Religious Research Association, Boston, 1999.

24. Guth et al., "Women Clergy"; Guth et al., *Bully Pulpit.*

25. See Guth et al., *Bully Pulpit,* and Olson, *Filled with Spirit.*

26. On this point see Guth et al., *Bully Pulpit.*

27. Olson, Crawford, and Guth.

28. See the feminization argument posited by James Davison Hunter and Kimon Howland Sargeant, "Religion and the Transformation of Public Culture," *Social Research* 60 (1993): 545–70.

29. Ibid. See also James Davison Hunter, *Culture Wars: The Struggle to Define America* (New York: Basic Books, 1991); Martin E. Marty, *Righteous Empire: The Protestant Experience in America* (New York: Dial Press, 1970); and Robert Wuthnow, *The Restructuring of American Religion: Society and Faith since World War II* (Princeton: Princeton University Press, 1988).

30. We would be remiss not to acknowledge the challenges that have been brought against the culture wars thesis, which could render the question of whether it would be exacerbated by the "feminization" of the clergy moot. Among others, see Paul J. DiMaggio, John H. Evans, and Bethany Bryson, "Have Americans' Social Attitudes Become More Polarized?" *American Journal of Sociology* 102 (1996): 690–755, and Rhys H. Williams, ed., *Cultural Wars in American Politics: Critical Reviews of a Popular Myth* (New York: Aldine, 1997).

31. Herbert Blumer, "Social Problems as Collective Behavior," *Social Problems* 18 (1971): 298–306.

32. Hans-Bernd Brosius and Gabriel Weimann, "Who Sets the Agenda? Agenda Setting as a Two-Step Flow," *Communication Research* 23 (1996): 561–80.

Chapter 5

1. Steven J. Rosenstone and John Mark Hansen, *Mobilization, Participation, and Democracy in America* (New York: Macmillan, 1993).

2. Ibid. Another important exception is James L. Guth, John C. Green, Corwin E. Smidt, Lyman A. Kellstedt, and Margaret M. Poloma, *The Bully Pulpit: The Politics of Protestant Clergy* (Lawrence, KS: University Press of Kansas, 1997). In this seminal work on the political behavior of Protestant clergy, Guth and his colleagues analyze the importance of clergy's issue agendas for their politics.

3. We coded the following issues as economic and social welfare concerns: child care, children, the disabled, economics, education, the elderly, health care, hunger, inner cities (lack of economic opportunity), poverty, socioeconomic gap, and welfare reform. We coded the following issues as discrimination concerns: abortion rights, AIDS, anti-Semitism, civil rights, discrimination, gender, homosexuality, human rights, intolerance, racism, and women.

4. Guth et al., *Bully Pulpit;* Harold E. Quinley, *The Prophetic Clergy: Social Activism among Protestant Ministers* (New York: Wiley, 1974).

5. H. Richard Niebuhr, *Christ and Culture* (New York: Harper and Row, 1951).

6. Nancy T. Ammerman, *Congregation and Community* (New Brunswick: Rutgers University Press, 1997); Nancy T. Ammerman, "Connecting Mainline Protestant Churches with Public Life," in Robert Wuthnow and John H. Evans, eds., *The Quiet Hand of God: Faith-Based Activism and the Public Role of Mainline Protestantism* (Berkeley: University of California Press, 2002); Mark Chaves, Helen M. Giesel, and William Tsitsos, "Religious Variations in Public Presence: Evidence from the National Congregations Study," in Wuthnow and Evans, eds., *Quiet Hand of God;* Ram A. Cnaan, *The Invisible Caring Hand: American Congregations and the Provision of Welfare* (New York: New York University Press, 2002); Ram A. Cnaan, *The Newer Deal: Social Work and Religion in Partnership* (New York: Columbia University Press, 1999); Virginia A. Hodgkinson and Murray S. Weitzman, *From Belief to Commitment: The Community Service Activities and Finances of Religious Congregations in the United States* (Washington, DC: Independent Sector, 1993); James R. Wood, *Leadership in Voluntary Organizations: The Controversy over Social Action in Protestant Churches* (New Brunswick: Rutgers University Press, 1981); Robert Wuthnow, *Acts of Compassion: Caring for Others and Helping Ourselves* (Princeton: Princeton University Press, 1991).

7. James F. Findlay, *Church People in the Struggle: The National Council of Churches and the Black Freedom Movement, 1950–1970* (New York: Oxford University Press, 1993); Michael B. Friedland, *Lift Up Your Voice Like a Trumpet: White Clergy and the Civil Rights and Antiwar Movements, 1954–1973* (Chapel Hill: University of North Carolina Press, 1998).

8. Sue E. S. Crawford, "Clergy at Work in the Secular City," Ph.D. diss., Indiana University, 1995.

9. Rosenstone and Hansen.

10. Ibid., 101–17.

11. Guth et al., *Bully Pulpit.*

12. Jackson W. Carroll, Barbara G. Wheeler, Daniel O. Aleshire, and Penny Long Marler, *Being There: Culture and Formation in Two Theological Schools* (New York: Oxford University Press, 1997); James L. Guth, "Reflections on the Status of Research on Clergy in Politics," in Sue E. S. Crawford and Laura R. Olson, eds., *Christian Clergy in American Politics* (Baltimore: Johns Hopkins University Press, 2001).

13. Rosenstone and Hansen.

14. Previous research has demonstrated that congregations are important units of analysis and that they take on meaningful and distinctive cultures of their own—and thus might have expectations for political action by their clergy. See Ammerman, *Congregation and Community,* and Penny Edgell Becker, *Con-*

gregations in Conflict: Cultural Models of Local Religious Life (New York: Cambridge University Press, 1999).

15. Mark Chaves, "Religious Congregations and Welfare Reform: Who Will Take Advantage of 'Charitable Choice'?" *American Sociological Review* 64 (1999): 836–46; Cnaan, *Invisible Caring Hand* and *Newer Deal;* Laura R. Olson, *Filled with Spirit and Power: Protestant Clergy in Politics* (Albany: State University of New York Press, 2000); Quinley.

16. Some observers argue that American religion resembles a competitive marketplace wherein houses of worship must actively compete for members. Thus it would be irrational for clergy who head declining congregations to engage in action that might alienate those congregants who remain. See Roger Finke and Rodney Stark, *The Churching of America, 1776–1990: Winners and Losers in Our Religious Economy* (New Brunswick: Rutgers University Press, 1992), for an extended discussion of this market-based logic.

17. See also Crawford, "Clergy at Work," and Sue E. S. Crawford and Laura R. Olson, "Clergy as Political Actors in Urban Contexts," in Crawford and Olson, eds., *Christian Clergy*. Examples of such groups that elicited some participation by the women we interviewed included the Milwaukee Innercity Congregations Allied for Hope, People of Indianapolis Seeking Employment and Development, Washington Interfaith Network, and Omaha Together One Community.

18. Crawford and Olson; Olson, *Filled with Spirit*.

19. Robert Huckfeldt, *Politics in Context: Assimilation and Conflict in Urban Neighborhoods* (New York: Agathon, 1986); Robert Huckfeldt, Paul Allen Beck, Russell J. Dalton, and Jeffrey Levine, "Political Environments, Cohesive Social Groups, and the Communication of Public Opinion," *American Journal of Political Science* 39 (1995): 1025–54; Sidney Verba, Kay Lehman Schlozman, and Henry E. Brady, *Voice and Equality: Civic Voluntarism in American Politics* (Cambridge, MA: Harvard University Press, 1995).

Chapter 6

1. James L. Guth, John C. Green, Corwin E. Smidt, Lyman A. Kellstedt, and Margaret M. Poloma, *The Bully Pulpit: The Politics of Protestant Clergy* (Lawrence, KS: University Press of Kansas, 1997), 147–53.

2. See also Sue E. S. Crawford, "Clergy at Work in the Secular City," Ph.D. diss., Indiana University, 1995.

3. A variety of other scholars have emphasized the importance of the less obviously political side of congregational activism. Among others, see Nancy T. Ammerman, *Congregation and Community* (New Brunswick: Rutgers University

Press, 1997); Nancy T. Ammerman, "Connecting Mainline Protestant Churches with Public Life," in Robert Wuthnow and John H. Evans, eds., *The Quiet Hand of God: Faith-Based Activism and the Public Role of Mainline Protestantism* (Berkeley: University of California Press, 2002); Mark Chaves, "Religious Congregations and Welfare Reform: Who Will Take Advantage of 'Charitable Choice'?" *American Sociological Review* 64 (1999): 836–46; Mark Chaves, Helen M. Giesel, and William Tsitsos, "Religious Variations in Public Presence: Evidence from the National Congregations Study," in Wuthnow and Evans, eds., *Quiet Hand of God;* Ram A. Cnaan, *The Invisible Caring Hand: American Congregations and the Provision of Welfare* (New York: New York University Press, 2002); Ram A. Cnaan, *The Newer Deal: Social Work and Religion in Partnership* (New York: Columbia University Press, 1999); Stephen Hart, *Cultural Dilemmas of Progressive Politics: Styles of Engagement among Grassroots Activists* (Chicago: University of Chicago Press, 2001); Virginia A. Hodgkinson and Murray S. Weitzman, *From Belief to Commitment: The Community Service Activities and Finances of Religious Congregations in the United States* (Washington, DC: Independent Sector, 1993); David A. Roozen, William McKinney, and Jackson W. Carroll, *Varieties of Religious Presence: Mission in Public Life* (New York: Pilgrim Press, 1984); James R. Wood, *Leadership in Voluntary Organizations: The Controversy over Social Action in Protestant Churches* (New Brunswick: Rutgers University Press, 1981); and Robert Wuthnow, *Acts of Compassion: Caring for Others and Helping Ourselves* (Princeton: Princeton University Press, 1991).

4. We define "urban" as working in a congregation that is located in a medium (population 50,000 to 100,000), large (100,000 to 500,000), or very large (more than 500,000) city. Clergy who specified working in a "farm or rural" community or "small town" were coded as such. The remainder of clergy report working in a small city (population 15,000 to 50,000), suburb of a large city, or suburb of a very large city.

5. Other differences between the survey taken from the four-city study and the national study are relatively minor. In several instances, the national survey and four-city survey do not include the same questions, particularly in the case of the approval measures. The reason for this discrepancy is that the national survey was conducted as part of a larger project involving numerous researchers, and space was not allotted for all of the measures we would have liked. Fortunately, most of the issues under consideration here are also available in the national survey and work well in the present analyses.

6. Melissa M. Deckman, Sue E. S. Crawford, Laura R. Olson, and John C. Green, "Clergy and the Politics of Gender: Women and Political Opportunity

in Mainline Protestant Churches," *Journal for the Scientific Study of Religion* 42 (2003): 621–32.

7. Ibid.

8. Ibid. In this previous research, we found that women clergy have a significantly higher mean score of political activity (they participate in 7.58 of a possible 24 different electoral and advocacy political activities) than do men clergy (whose mean score is 6.54). This evidence runs counter to the gender-gap expectation so prevalent in research about men and women in politics more broadly, which finds that men are more likely to participate in politics than women. Our finding strongly suggests that despite concerns about discrimination—or perhaps because of them—women clergy are a very politicized group of professionals.

9. Saul D. Alinsky, *Reveille for Radicals* (New York: Random House, 1946); Jim Rooney, *Organizing the South Bronx* (Albany: State University of New York Press, 1995).

10. See Chaves, "Religious Congregations," and Cnaan, *Invisible Caring Hand* and *Newer Deal.*

11. Deckman et al.

12. Ibid.

13. Ibid.

14. Crawford; Sue E. S. Crawford and Laura R. Olson, "Clergy as Political Actors in Urban Contexts," in Sue E. S. Crawford and Laura R. Olson, eds., *Christian Clergy in American Politics* (Baltimore: Johns Hopkins University Press, 2001); Laura R. Olson, *Filled with Spirit and Power: Protestant Clergy in Politics* (Albany: State University of New York Press, 2000).

15. For discussions of clergy involvement in the Near Eastside and Mapleton-Fall Creek neighborhoods of Indianapolis, see Crawford and Richard Kordesh, "Democracy from Above and Below: The Reorganization of Neighborhood Politics," Ph.D. diss., Indiana University, 1986.

16. See Crawford; Crawford and Olson; and Olson, *Filled with Spirit.*

17. See James L. Adams, *The Growing Church Lobby in Washington* (Grand Rapids: Eerdmans, 1970); Jeffrey K. Hadden, *The Gathering Storm in the Churches* (Garden City, NY: Doubleday, 1969); and Norman B. Koller and Joseph D. Retzer, "The Sounds of Silence Revisited," *Sociological Analysis* 41 (1980): 155–61.

Chapter 7

1. Our findings regarding activism are echoed in Melissa M. Deckman, Sue E. S. Crawford, Laura R. Olson, and John C. Green, "Clergy and the Politics of Gender: Women and Political Opportunity in Mainline Protestant

Churches," *Journal for the Scientific Study of Religion* 42 (2003): 621–32; and Paul A. Djupe and Christopher P. Gilbert, *The Prophetic Pulpit: Clergy, Churches, and Communities in American Politics* (Lanham, MD: Rowman and Littlefield, 2003).

2. Nancy T. Ammerman, *Congregation and Community* (New Brunswick: Rutgers University Press, 1997); Nancy T. Ammerman, "Connecting Mainline Protestant Churches with Public Life," in Robert Wuthnow and John H. Evans, eds., *The Quiet Hand of God: Faith-Based Activism and the Public Role of Mainline Protestantism* (Berkeley: University of California Press, 2002); Mark Chaves, Helen M. Giesel, and William Tsitsos, "Religious Variations in Public Presence: Evidence from the National Congregations Study," in Wuthnow and Evans, eds., *Quiet Hand of God;* Ram A. Cnaan, *The Invisible Caring Hand: American Congregations and the Provision of Welfare* (New York: New York University Press, 2002); Ram A. Cnaan, *The Newer Deal: Social Work and Religion in Partnership* (New York: Columbia University Press, 1999); Stephen Hart, *Cultural Dilemmas of Progressive Politics: Styles of Engagement among Grassroots Activists* (Chicago: University of Chicago Press, 2001); Laura R. Olson, *Filled with Spirit and Power: Protestant Clergy in Politics* (Albany: State University of New York Press, 2000); Laura R. Olson, "Mainline Protestant Washington Offices and the Political Lives of Clergy," in Wuthnow and Evans, eds., *Quiet Hand of God;* Richard Parker, "Progressive Politics and Visions—and, Uh, Well . . . God," in E. J. Dionne, Jr., and John J. DiIulio, Jr., eds., *What's God Got to Do with the American Experiment?* (Washington, DC: The Brookings Institution, 2000); David A. Roozen, William McKinney, and Jackson W. Carroll, *Varieties of Religious Presence: Mission in Public Life* (New York: Pilgrim Press, 1984); Robert Wuthnow, *Acts of Compassion: Caring for Others and Helping Ourselves* (Princeton: Princeton University Press, 1991).

3. Sue E. S. Crawford, "Clergy at Work in the Secular City," Ph.D. diss., Indiana University, 1995; Sue E. S. Crawford and Laura R. Olson, "Clergy as Political Actors in Urban Contexts," in Sue E. S. Crawford and Laura R. Olson, eds., *Christian Clergy in American Politics* (Baltimore: Johns Hopkins University Press, 2001); Olson, *Filled with Spirit.*

4. See, for example, Sidney Verba, Kay Lehman Schlozman, and Henry E. Brady, *Voice and Equality: Civic Voluntarism in American Politics* (Cambridge, MA: Harvard University Press, 1995).

5. Anthony Downs, *An Economic Theory of Democracy* (New York: Harper, 1957); Stephen Knack, "Civic Norms, Social Sanctions, and Voter Turnout," *Rationality and Society* 4 (1992): 133–56; Paul E. Meehl, "The Selfish Voter Paradox and the Thrown Away Vote Argument," *American Political Science Review* 71

(1977): 11–30. In contrast, much attention has been given to norms or principles in analyses of collective action dilemmas and state legitimacy. See Sue E. S. Crawford and Elinor Ostrom, "A Grammar of Institutions," *American Political Science Review* 89 (1995): 582–600.

6. James L. Guth, John C. Green, Corwin E. Smidt, Lyman A. Kellstedt, and Margaret M. Poloma, *The Bully Pulpit: The Politics of Protestant Clergy* (Lawrence, KS: University Press of Kansas, 1997).

7. Ted G. Jelen, *The Political World of the Clergy* (Westport: Praeger, 1993).

8. Some extant research suggests that women clergy emphasize subjective work-related rewards more than their male counterparts. This finding would help to explain, perhaps, why we find that clergywomen are less politically constrained than might be expected. See Joy Charlton, "Women and Clergywomen," *Sociology of Religion* 61 (2000): 419–24; Martha Long Ice, *Clergy Women and Their Worldviews: Calling for a New Age* (Westport: Praeger, 1987); Elaine M. McDuff, "The Gender Paradox in Work Satisfaction and the Protestant Clergy," *Sociology of Religion* 62 (2001): 1–21; Elaine M. McDuff and Charles W. Mueller, "Social Support and Compensating Differentials in the Protestant Ministry: Gender Differences in Two Protestant Denominations," *Review of Religious Research* 40 (1999): 307–29; Jo Phelan, "The Paradox of the Contented Female Worker: An Assessment of Alternative Explanations," *Social Psychology Quarterly* 57 (1994): 95–107; Carl J. Schneider and Dorothy Schneider, *In Their Own Right: The History of American Clergywomen* (New York: Crossroad, 1997); and Rodney Stark and Roger Finke, *Acts of Faith: Explaining the Human Side of Religion* (Berkeley: University of California Press, 2000).

9. Ernest Q. Campbell and Thomas F. Pettigrew, *Christians in Racial Crisis: A Study of Little Rock's Ministry* (Washington, DC: Public Affairs Press, 1959); Jeffrey K. Hadden, *The Gathering Storm in the Churches* (Garden City, NY: Doubleday, 1969); Harold E. Quinley, *The Prophetic Clergy: Social Activism among Protestant Ministers* (New York: Wiley, 1974).

10. See Penny Edgell Becker, *Congregations in Conflict: Cultural Models of Local Religious Life* (New York: Cambridge University Press, 1999); Crawford and Olson; Olson, *Filled with Spirit.*

11. E. Wilbur Bock, "The Female Clergy: A Case of Professional Marginality," *American Journal of Sociology* 72 (1967): 531–39; Jackson W. Carroll, Barbara Hargrove, and Adair T. Lummis, *Women of the Cloth: A New Opportunity for the Churches* (San Francisco: Harper and Row, 1983); Patricia M. Y. Chang, "Female Clergy in the Contemporary Protestant Church: A Current Assessment," *Journal for the Scientific Study of Religion* 36 (1997): 565–73; Ice; Edward C. Lehman, *Women Clergy: Breaking through Gender Barriers* (New Brunswick: Transaction,

1985); Frederick W. Schmidt, *A Still Small Voice: Women, Ordination, and the Church* (Syracuse: Syracuse University Press, 1996); Barbara Brown Zikmund, Adair T. Lummis, and Patricia Mei Yin Chang, *Clergy Women: An Uphill Calling* (Louisville: Westminster John Knox, 1998).

12. Martin E. Marty, *Politics, Religion, and the Common Good: Advancing a Distinctly American Conversation about Religion's Role in Our Shared Life* (San Francisco: Jossey-Bass, 2000).

13. See R. Marie Griffith, "The Generous Side of Christian Faith: The Successes and Challenges of Mainline Women's Groups," in Wuthnow and Evans, eds., *Quiet Hand of God,* and Olson, "Mainline Protestant Washington Offices."

14. The small amount of research that has been done on Pentecostal and African American Protestant clergywomen amounts to Charles H. Barfoot and Gerald T. Sheppard, "Prophetic vs. Priestly Religion: The Changing Role of Women Clergy in Classical Pentecostal Churches," *Review of Religious Research* 22 (1980): 2–17; Cheryl Townsend Gilkes, "Together and in Harness: Women's Traditions in the Sanctified Church," in Micheline R. Malson, Elisabeth Mudimbe-Boyi, Jean F. O'Barr, and Mary Wyer, eds., *Black Women in America: Social Science Perspectives* (Chicago: University of Chicago Press, 1990); Elaine J. Lawless, *Handmaidens of the Lord: Pentecostal Women Preachers and Traditional Religion* (Philadelphia: University of Pennsylvania Press, 1988); and Cheryl J. Sanders, "History of Women in the Pentecostal Movement," *Cyberjournal for Pentecostal-Charismatic Research* 2 (1997): 1–13.

15. Richard A. Schoenherr, *Goodbye Father: The Celibate Male Priesthood and the Future of the Catholic Church* (New York: Oxford University Press, 2002).

16. Karen M. Kaufmann and John R. Petrocik, "The Changing Politics of American Men: Understanding the Sources of the Gender Gap," *American Journal of Political Science* 43 (1999): 864–87; Margaret C. Trevor, "Political Socialization, Party Identification, and the Gender Gap," *Public Opinion Quarterly* 63 (1999): 62–78; Susan Welch, "Women as Political Animals? A Test of Some Explanations for Male-Female Political Participation Differences," *American Journal of Political Science* 21 (1977): 711–30.

17. Deckman et al.

18. We argue this point in Sue E. S. Crawford, Laura R. Olson, and Melissa M. Deckman, "Understanding the Mobilization of Professionals," *Nonprofit and Voluntary Sector Quarterly* 30 (2001): 321–50.

19. Benjamin R. Barber, *Strong Democracy: Participatory Politics for a New Age* (Berkeley: University of California Press, 1984); Kate Millett, *Sexual Politics* (New York: Avon, 1970); Carole Pateman, *Participation and Democratic Theory* (New York: Cambridge University Press, 1970); Verba, Schlozman, and Brady.

20. James Davison Hunter and Kimon Howland Sargeant, "Religion and the Transformation of Public Culture," *Social Research* 60 (1993): 545–70.

21. James L. Adams, *The Growing Church Lobby in Washington* (Grand Rapids: Eerdmans, 1970); Hadden; Norman B. Koller and Joseph D. Retzer, "The Sounds of Silence Revisited," *Sociological Analysis* 41 (1980): 155–61.

22. Roger Finke and Rodney Stark, *The Churching of America, 1776–1990: Winners and Losers in Our Religious Economy* (New Brunswick: Rutgers University Press, 1992).

23. Phil Zuckerman, *Strife in the Sanctuary: Religious Schism in a Jewish Community* (Walnut Creek, CA: Alta Mira Press, 1999).

24. On numeric decline, see Andrew Kohut, John C. Green, Scott Keeter, and Robert C. Toth, *The Diminishing Divide: Religion's Changing Role in American Politics* (Washington, DC: The Brookings Institution, 2000). On future vibrancy, see Sylvia Barack Fishman, *Jewish Life and American Culture* (Albany: State University of New York Press, 2000); Robert Wuthnow, "Beyond Quiet Influence? Possibilities for the Protestant Mainline," in Wuthnow and Evans, eds., *Quiet Hand of God;* and Robert Wuthnow, "The Moral Minority," *The American Prospect* 11 (22 May 2000).

Bibliography

Adams, James L. *The Growing Church Lobby in Washington.* Grand Rapids: Eerdmans, 1970.

Alinsky, Saul D. *Reveille for Radicals.* New York: Random House, 1946.

Ammerman, Nancy T. *Congregation and Community.* New Brunswick: Rutgers University Press, 1997.

———. "Connecting Mainline Protestant Churches with Public Life." In Robert Wuthnow and John H. Evans, eds., *The Quiet Hand of God: Faith-Based Activism and the Public Role of Mainline Protestantism.* Berkeley: University of California Press, 2002.

Andersen, Kristi. "Working Women and Political Participation, 1952–1972." *American Journal of Political Science* 19 (1975): 439–55.

Barber, Benjamin R. *Strong Democracy: Participatory Politics for a New Age.* Berkeley: University of California Press, 1984.

Barfoot, Charles H., and Gerald T. Sheppard. "Prophetic vs. Priestly Religion: The Changing Role of Women Clergy in Classical Pentecostal Churches." *Review of Religious Research* 22 (1980): 2–17.

Becker, Penny Edgell. *Congregations in Conflict: Cultural Models of Local Religious Life.* New York: Cambridge University Press, 1999.

Bingham, Clara. *Women on the Hill: Challenging the Culture of Congress.* New York: Times Books, 1997.

Blumer, Herbert. "Social Problems as Collective Behavior." *Social Problems* 18 (1971): 298–306.

Bock, E. Wilbur. "The Female Clergy: A Case of Professional Marginality." *American Journal of Sociology* 72 (1967): 531–39.

Bourque, Susan, and Jean Grossholtz. "Politics as an Unnatural Practice: Political Science Looks at Female Participation." *Politics and Society* 4 (1974): 255–66.

Boyd, Sandra Hughes. "A Woman's Journey toward Priesthood: An Autobiographical Study from the 1950s through the 1980s." In Catherine M. Prelinger, ed., *Episcopal Women: Gender, Spirituality, and Commitment in an American Mainline Denomination.* New York: Oxford University Press, 1992.

Brosius, Hans-Bernd, and Gabriel Weimann. "Who Sets the Agenda? Agenda Setting as a Two-Step Flow." *Communication Research* 23 (1996): 561–80.

Burns, Nancy, Kay Lehman Schlozman, and Sidney Verba. *The Private Roots of Public Action: Gender, Equality, and Political Participation.* Cambridge, MA: Harvard University Press, 2001.

Cadge, Wendy. "Vital Conflicts: The Mainline Protestant Denominations Debate Homosexuality." In Robert Wuthnow and John H. Evans, eds., *The Quiet Hand of God: Faith-Based Activism and the Public Role of Mainline Protestantism.* Berkeley: University of California Press, 2002.

Campbell, Ernest Q., and Thomas F. Pettigrew. *Christians in Racial Crisis: A Study of Little Rock's Ministry.* Washington, DC: Public Affairs Press, 1959.

Carroll, Jackson W., Barbara Hargrove, and Adair T. Lummis. *Women of the Cloth: A New Opportunity for the Churches.* San Francisco: Harper and Row, 1983.

Carroll, Jackson W., Barbara G. Wheeler, Daniel O. Aleshire, and Penny Long Marler. *Being There: Culture and Formation in Two Theological Schools.* New York: Oxford University Press, 1997.

Cavendish, James C. "To March or Not to March: Clergy Mobilization Strategies and Grassroots Antidrug Activism." In Sue E. S. Crawford and Laura R. Olson, eds., *Christian Clergy in American Politics.* Baltimore: Johns Hopkins University Press, 2001.

Chang, Patricia M. Y. "Female Clergy in the Contemporary Protestant Church: A Current Assessment." *Journal for the Scientific Study of Religion* 36 (1997): 565–73.

Charlton, Joy. "What It Means to Go First: Clergywomen of the Pioneer Generation." Presented at the annual meeting of the Society for the Scientific Study of Religion, St. Louis, 1995.

———. "Women and Clergywomen." *Sociology of Religion* 61 (2000): 419–24.

Chaves, Mark. *Ordaining Women: Culture and Conflict in Religious Organizations.* Cambridge, MA: Harvard University Press, 1997.

———. "Religious Congregations and Welfare Reform: Who Will Take Advantage of 'Charitable Choice'?" *American Sociological Review* 64 (1999): 836–46.

Chaves, Mark, Helen M. Giesel, and William Tsitsos. "Religious Variations in Public Presence: Evidence from the National Congregations Study." In Robert Wuthnow and John H. Evans, eds., *The Quiet Hand of God: Faith-*

Based Activism and the Public Role of Mainline Protestantism. Berkeley: University of California Press, 2002.

Clark, Cal, and Janet Clark. "Models of Gender and Political Participation in the United States." *Women and Politics* 6 (1986): 5–25.

Cnaan, Ram A. *The Invisible Caring Hand: American Congregations and the Provision of Welfare.* New York: New York University Press, 2002.

———. *The Newer Deal: Social Work and Religion in Partnership.* New York: Columbia University Press, 1999.

Coburn, Carol K., and Martha Smith. *Spirited Lives: How Nuns Shaped Catholic Culture and American Life, 1836–1920.* Chapel Hill: University of North Carolina Press, 1999.

Cochran, Larry. *The Sense of Vocation: A Study of Career and Life Development.* Albany: State University of New York Press, 1990.

Conway, M. Margaret. *Political Participation in the United States,* 2nd ed. Washington, DC: CQ Press, 1991.

Coombs, Marie T., and Francis K. Nemeck. *Called by God: A Theology of Vocation and Lifelong Commitment.* Collegeville, MN: Liturgical Press, 1992.

Crawford, Sue E. S. "Clergy at Work in the Secular City." Ph.D. diss., Indiana University, 1995.

Crawford, Sue E. S., Melissa M. Deckman, and Christi J. Braun. "Gender and the Political Choices of Women Clergy." In Sue E. S. Crawford and Laura R. Olson, eds., *Christian Clergy in American Politics.* Baltimore: Johns Hopkins University Press, 2001.

Crawford, Sue E. S., and Kristin Kadleck. "The Workplace Experiences of Women Clergy: Does the Personal Become Political?" Presented at the annual meeting of the Religious Research Association, Boston, 1999.

Crawford, Sue E. S., and Laura R. Olson. "Clergy as Political Actors in Urban Contexts." In Sue E. S. Crawford and Laura R. Olson, eds., *Christian Clergy in American Politics.* Baltimore: Johns Hopkins University Press, 2001.

Crawford, Sue E. S., Laura R. Olson, and Melissa M. Deckman. "Understanding the Mobilization of Professionals." *Nonprofit and Voluntary Sector Quarterly* 30 (2001): 321–50.

Crawford, Sue E. S., and Elinor Ostrom. "A Grammar of Institutions." *American Political Science Review* 89 (1995): 582–600.

Culver, Virginia. "Methodists See More Female Clergy Depart." *The Denver Post,* 26 February 1999: B5.

Daly, Mary. *The Church and the Second Sex.* New York: Harper and Row, 1968.

Deckman, Melissa M. *School Board Battles: The Christian Right in Local Politics.* Washington, DC: Georgetown University Press, 2004.

Deckman, Melissa M., Sue E. S. Crawford, Laura R. Olson, and John C. Green. "Clergy and the Politics of Gender: Women and Political Opportunity in Mainline Protestant Churches." *Journal for the Scientific Study of Religion* 42 (2003): 621–32.

DiMaggio, Paul J., John H. Evans, and Bethany Bryson. "Have Americans' Social Attitudes Become More Polarized?" *American Journal of Sociology* 102 (1996): 690–755.

Dionne, E. J., and Ming Hsu Chen, eds. *Sacred Places, Civic Purposes: Should Government Help Faith-based Charity?* Washington, DC: The Brookings Institution, 2001.

Djupe, Paul A., and Christopher P. Gilbert. *The Prophetic Pulpit: Clergy, Churches, and Communities in American Politics.* Lanham, MD: Rowman and Littlefield, 2003.

Downs, Anthony. *An Economic Theory of Democracy.* New York: Harper, 1957.

Durkheim, Émile. *The Elementary Forms of the Religious Life.* 1912. Reprint, New York: Free Press, 1995.

Duverger, Maurice. *The Political Role of Women.* New York: UNESCO, 1955.

Easton, David. *A Systems Analysis of Political Life.* Chicago: University of Chicago Press, 1979.

Findlay, James F. *Church People in the Struggle: The National Council of Churches and the Black Freedom Movement, 1950–1970.* New York: Oxford University Press, 1993.

Finke, Roger, and Rodney Stark. *The Churching of America, 1776–1990: Winners and Losers in Our Religious Economy.* New Brunswick: Rutgers University Press, 1992.

Finlay, Barbara. "Do Men and Women Have Different Goals for Ministry? Evidence from Seminarians." *Sociology of Religion* 57 (1996): 311–18.

Fishman, Sylvia Barack. *Jewish Life and American Culture.* Albany: State University of New York Press, 2000.

Fowler, Robert Booth, Allen D. Hertzke, and Laura R. Olson. *Religion and Politics in America: Faith, Culture, and Strategic Choices,* 2nd ed. Boulder: Westview, 1999.

Friedan, Betty. *The Feminine Mystique.* New York: Dell, 1963.

Friedland, Michael B. *Lift Up Your Voice Like a Trumpet: White Clergy and the Civil Rights and Antiwar Movements, 1954–1973.* Chapel Hill: University of North Carolina Press, 1998.

Gallup Organization. *Gallup Poll Trends: "Most Important Problem."* 1999. http://www.gallup.com/poll/trends/ptproblem.asp.

Giele, Janet Zollinger. *Two Paths to Women's Equality: Temperance, Suffrage, and the Origins of Modern Feminism.* Old Tappan, NJ: Twayne, 1995.

Gilbert, Christopher P. *The Impact of Churches on Political Behavior: An Empirical Study.* Westport: Greenwood Press, 1993.

Gilkes, Cheryl Townsend. "Together and in Harness: Women's Traditions in the Sanctified Church." In Micheline R. Malson, Elisabeth Mudimbe-Boyi, Jean F. O'Barr, and Mary Wyer, eds., *Black Women in America: Social Science Perspectives.* Chicago: University of Chicago Press, 1990.

Gonzalez, Jennifer. "Hitting the Stained Glass Ceiling." *The Cleveland Plain Dealer* 12 December 1998: 1F.

Griffith, R. Marie. "The Generous Side of Christian Faith: The Successes and Challenges of Mainline Women's Groups." In Robert Wuthnow and John H. Evans, eds., *The Quiet Hand of God: Faith-Based Activism and the Public Role of Mainline Protestantism.* Berkeley: University of California Press, 2002.

Guth, James L. "Reflections on the Status of Research on Clergy in Politics." In Sue E. S. Crawford and Laura R. Olson, eds., *Christian Clergy in American Politics.* Baltimore: Johns Hopkins University Press, 2001.

Guth, James L., John C. Green, Corwin E. Smidt, and Lyman A. Kellstedt. "Women Clergy and the Political Transformation of Mainline Protestantism." Presented at the annual meeting of the Social Science History Association, Atlanta, 1994.

Guth, James L., John C. Green, Corwin E. Smidt, Lyman A. Kellstedt, and Margaret M. Poloma. *The Bully Pulpit: The Politics of Protestant Clergy.* Lawrence, KS: University Press of Kansas, 1997.

Hadaway, C. Kirk, Penny Long Marler, and Mark Chaves. "What the Polls Don't Show: A Closer Look at U.S. Church Attendance." *American Sociological Review* 58 (1993): 741–52.

Hadden, Jeffrey K. *The Gathering Storm in the Churches.* Garden City, NY: Doubleday, 1969.

Hart, Stephen. *Cultural Dilemmas of Progressive Politics: Styles of Engagement among Grassroots Activists.* Chicago: University of Chicago Press, 2001.

Hertzke, Allen D. *Representing God in Washington: The Role of Religious Lobbies in the American Polity.* Knoxville: University of Tennessee Press, 1988.

Hochschild, Arlie. *The Second Shift: Working Parents and the Revolution at Home.* New York: Viking Press, 1989.

Hodgkinson, Virginia A., and Murray S. Weitzman. *From Belief to Commitment: The Community Service Activities and Finances of Religious Congregations in the United States.* Washington, DC: Independent Sector, 1993.

Hofrenning, Daniel J. B. *In Washington but Not of It: The Prophetic Politics of Religious Lobbyists.* Philadelphia: Temple University Press, 1995.

Huckfeldt, Robert. *Politics in Context: Assimilation and Conflict in Urban Neighborhoods.* New York: Agathon, 1986.

Huckfeldt, Robert, Paul Allen Beck, Russell J. Dalton, and Jeffrey Levine. "Political Environments, Cohesive Social Groups, and the Communication of Public Opinion." *American Journal of Political Science* 39 (1995): 1025–54.

Huckfeldt, Robert, and John Sprague. *Citizens, Politics, and Social Communication: Information and Influence in an Election Campaign.* New York: Cambridge University Press, 1995.

Hunter, James Davison. *Before the Shooting Begins: Searching for Democracy in America's Culture War.* New York: Free Press, 1994.

———. *Culture Wars: The Struggle to Define America.* New York: Basic Books, 1991.

Hunter, James Davison, and Kimon Howland Sargeant. "Religion and the Transformation of Public Culture." *Social Research* 60 (1993): 545–70.

Ice, Martha Long. *Clergy Women and Their Worldviews: Calling for a New Age.* Westport: Praeger, 1987.

Iyengar, Shanto, and Donald R. Kinder. *News That Matters: Television and American Opinion.* Chicago: University of Chicago Press, 1987.

Jelen, Ted G. "Notes for a Theory of Clergy as Political Leaders." In Sue E. S. Crawford and Laura R. Olson, eds., *Christian Clergy in American Politics.* Baltimore: Johns Hopkins University Press, 2001.

———. *The Political World of the Clergy.* Westport: Praeger, 1993.

John Paul II. *Ordinatio Sacerdotalis: Apostolic Letter on Reserving Priestly Ordination to Men Alone.* Boston: Pauline Books, 1994.

Kahn, Kim Fridkin. *The Political Consequences of Being a Woman: How Stereotypes Influence the Conduct and Consequences of Political Campaigns.* New York: Columbia University Press, 1996.

Kanter, Rosabeth Moss. *Men and Women of the Corporation,* 2nd ed. New York: Basic Books, 1993.

Kathlene, Lyn. "Power and Influence in State Legislative Policy Making: The Interaction of Gender and Position in Committee Hearing Debates." *American Political Science Review* 43 (1994): 864–87.

Katz, Elihu, and Paul F. Lazarsfeld. *Personal Influence: The Part Played by People in the Flow of Mass Communications.* New York: Free Press, 1955.

Katzenstein, Mary Fainsod. *Faithful and Fearless: Moving Feminist Protest inside the Church and Military.* Princeton: Princeton University Press, 1998.

Kaufmann, Karen M., and John R. Petrocik. "The Changing Politics of American Men: Understanding the Sources of the Gender Gap." *American Journal of Political Science* 43 (1999): 864–87.

Kaylin, Lucy. *For the Love of God: The Faith and Future of the American Nun.* New York: William Morrow, 2000.

Keller, Rosemary Skinner, and Rosemary Radford Ruether, eds. *In Our Own Voices: Four Centuries of American Women's Religious Writing.* Louisville: Westminster John Knox, 1995.

———, eds. *Women and Religion in America.* San Francisco: Harper and Row, 1981.

Kelly, Rita Mae. "Offensive Men, Defensive Women: Sexual Harassment, Leadership, and Management." In Georgia Duerst-Lahti and Rita Mae Kelly, eds., *Gender Power, Leadership, and Governance.* Ann Arbor: University of Michigan Press, 1995.

Kingdon, John W. *Agendas, Alternatives, and Public Policies,* 2nd ed. New York: Harper Collins, 1995.

Knack, Stephen. "Civic Norms, Social Sanctions, and Voter Turnout." *Rationality and Society* 4 (1992): 133–56.

Kohut, Andrew, John C. Green, Scott Keeter, and Robert C. Toth. *The Diminishing Divide: Religion's Changing Role in American Politics.* Washington, DC: The Brookings Institution, 2000.

Koller, Norman B., and Joseph D. Retzer. "The Sounds of Silence Revisited." *Sociological Analysis* 41 (1980): 155–61.

Kordesh, Richard. "Democracy from Above and Below: The Reorganization of Neighborhood Politics." Ph.D. diss., Indiana University, 1986.

Lasswell, Harold. *Politics: Who Gets What, When, How.* New York: World, 1958.

Lawless, Elaine J. *Handmaidens of the Lord: Pentecostal Women Preachers and Traditional Religion.* Philadelphia: University of Pennsylvania Press, 1988.

Lehman, Edward C. *Women Clergy: Breaking through Gender Barriers.* New Brunswick: Transaction, 1985.

Liebman, Charles S., and Steven M. Cohen. *Two Worlds of Judaism: The Israeli and American Experiences.* New Haven: Yale University Press, 1990.

Lienesch, Michael. *Redeeming America: Piety and Politics in the New Christian Right.* Chapel Hill: University of North Carolina Press, 1993.

Manning, Christel. *God Gave Us the Right: Conservative Catholic, Evangelical Protestant, and Orthodox Jewish Women Grapple with Feminism.* New Brunswick: Rutgers University Press, 1999.

Marty, Martin E. *Politics, Religion, and the Common Good: Advancing a Distinctly American Conversation about Religion's Role in Our Shared Life.* San Francisco: Jossey-Bass, 2000.

————. *Righteous Empire: The Protestant Experience in America.* New York: Dial Press, 1970.

McCord, Julia. "Pastor's Trial May Be Crossroads for Church." *The Omaha World-Herald* 8 March 1997: 1A.

McDuff, Elaine M. "The Gender Paradox in Work Satisfaction and the Protestant Clergy." *Sociology of Religion* 62 (2001): 1–21.

McDuff, Elaine M., and Charles W. Mueller. "Social Support and Compensating Differentials in the Protestant Ministry: Gender Differences in Two Protestant Denominations." *Review of Religious Research* 40 (1999): 307–29.

McGlen, Nancy. "The Impact of Parenthood on Political Participation." *Western Political Quarterly* 33 (1980): 297–313.

McGlen, Nancy, Karen O'Connor, Laura van Assendelft, and Wendy Gunther-Canada. *Women, Politics, and American Society,* 3rd ed. New York: Longman, 2002.

Meehl, Paul E. "The Selfish Voter Paradox and the Thrown Away Vote Argument." *American Political Science Review* 71 (1977): 11–30.

Millett, Kate. *Sexual Politics.* New York: Avon, 1970.

Morris, Aldon D. *The Origins of the Civil Rights Movement: Black Communities Organizing for Change.* New York: Free Press, 1984.

Nesbitt, Paula. "Clergy Feminization: Controlled Labor or Transformative Change?" *Journal for the Scientific Study of Religion* 36 (1997): 585–98.

Niebuhr, Gustav. "Following Mothers, Women Heed Call to Nation's Pulpits." *The New York Times* 25 April 1999: A1.

Niebuhr, H. Richard. *Christ and Culture.* New York: Harper and Row, 1951.

Norrander, Barbara, and Clyde Wilcox. "The Geography of Gender Power: Women in State Legislatures." In Sue Thomas and Clyde Wilcox, eds., *Women and Elective Office: Past, Present, and Future.* New York: Oxford University Press, 1998.

Olson, Laura R. *Filled with Spirit and Power: Protestant Clergy in Politics.* Albany: State University of New York Press, 2000.

————. "Mainline Protestant Washington Offices and the Political Lives of Clergy." In Robert Wuthnow and John H. Evans, eds., *The Quiet Hand of God: Faith-Based Activism and the Public Role of Mainline Protestantism.* Berkeley: University of California Press, 2002.

Olson, Laura R., Sue E. S. Crawford, and James L. Guth. "Changing Issue Agendas of Women Clergy." *Journal for the Scientific Study of Religion* 39 (2000): 140–53.

Parker, Richard. "Progressive Politics and Visions—and, Uh, Well . . . God." In E. J. Dionne, Jr., and John J. DiIulio, Jr., eds., *What's God Got to Do with the American Experiment?* Washington, DC: The Brookings Institution, 2000.

Pateman, Carole. *Participation and Democratic Theory.* New York: Cambridge University Press, 1970.

"Perspectives." *Newsweek* 30 October 2000: 31.

Phelan, Jo. "The Paradox of the Contented Female Worker: An Assessment of Alternative Explanations." *Social Psychology Quarterly* 57 (1994): 95–107.

Quinley, Harold E. *The Prophetic Clergy: Social Activism among Protestant Ministers.* New York: Wiley, 1974.

Quiñonez, Lora Ann, and Mary Daniel Turner. *The Transformation of American Catholic Sisters.* Philadelphia: Temple University Press, 1992.

Rooney, Jim. *Organizing the South Bronx.* Albany: State University of New York Press, 1995.

Roozen, David A., William McKinney, and Jackson W. Carroll. *Varieties of Religious Presence: Mission in Public Life.* New York: Pilgrim Press, 1984.

Rosenstone, Steven J., and John Mark Hansen. *Mobilization, Participation, and Democracy in America.* New York: Macmillan, 1993.

Samuels, Suzanne Uttaro. *Fetal Rights, Women's Rights: Gender Equality in the Workplace.* Madison: University of Wisconsin Press, 1995.

Sanders, Cheryl J. "History of Women in the Pentecostal Movement." *Cyberjournal for Pentecostal-Charismatic Research* 2 (1997): 1–13.

Sapiro, Virginia. *The Political Integration of Women: Roles, Socialization, and Politics.* Urbana: University of Illinois Press, 1983.

Schlozman, Kay Lehman, Nancy Burns, and Sidney Verba. "Gender and the Pathways to Participation: The Role of Resources." *Journal of Politics* 56 (1994): 963–90.

———. "'What Happened at Work Today?' A Multistage Model of Gender, Employment, and Political Participation." *Journal of Politics* 61 (1999): 29–53.

Schmidt, Frederick W. *A Still Small Voice: Women, Ordination, and the Church.* Syracuse: Syracuse University Press, 1996.

Schneider, Carl J., and Dorothy Schneider. *In Their Own Right: The History of American Clergywomen.* New York: Crossroad, 1997.

Schoenherr, Richard A. *Goodbye Father: The Celibate Male Priesthood and the Future of the Catholic Church.* New York: Oxford University Press, 2002.

Schoenherr, Richard A., and Lawrence A. Young. *Full Pews and Empty Altars: Demographics of the Priest Shortage in United States Catholic Dioceses.* Madison: University of Wisconsin Press, 1993.

Sigel, Roberta S. *Ambition and Accommodation: How Women View Gender Relations.* Chicago: University of Chicago Press, 1996.

"Southern Baptist Convention Passes Resolution Opposing Women as Pastors." *The New York Times* 15 June 2000: A18.

Stanton, Elizabeth Cady, Susan B. Anthony, and Matilda Joslyn Gage, eds. *History of Woman Suffrage,* Vol. 1. Rochester: Charles Mann, 1881.

Stark, Rodney, and Roger Finke. *Acts of Faith: Explaining the Human Side of Religion.* Berkeley: University of California Press, 2000.

Stark, Rodney, Bruce D. Foster, Charles Y. Glock, and Harold E. Quinley. *Wayward Shepherds: Prejudice and the Protestant Clergy.* New York: Harper and Row, 1971.

Steensland, Brian. "The Hydra and the Swords: Social Welfare and Mainline Advocacy, 1964–2000." In Robert Wuthnow and John H. Evans, eds., *The Quiet Hand of God: Faith-Based Activism and the Public Role of Mainline Protestantism.* Berkeley: University of California Press, 2002.

Stevens, Lesley. "Different Voice/Different Voices: Anglican Women in Ministry." *Review of Religious Research* 30 (1989): 262–75.

Stiehm, Judith Hicks. *Arms and the Enlisted Woman.* Philadelphia: Temple University Press, 1989.

Trevor, Margaret C. "Political Socialization, Party Identification, and the Gender Gap." *Public Opinion Quarterly* 63 (1999): 62–78.

The United Methodist Church. *The Book of Discipline 2000.* Nashville: Abingdon Press, 2000.

Verba, Sidney, and Norman H. Nie. *Participation in America: Political Democracy and Social Equality.* Chicago: University of Chicago Press, 1972.

Verba, Sidney, Kay Lehman Schlozman, and Henry E. Brady. *Voice and Equality: Civic Voluntarism in American Politics.* Cambridge, MA: Harvard University Press, 1995.

Verter, Bradford. "Furthering the Freedom Struggle: Racial Justice Activism in the Churches since the Civil Rights Era." In Robert Wuthnow and John H. Evans, eds., *The Quiet Hand of God: Faith-Based Activism and the Public Role of Mainline Protestantism.* Berkeley: University of California Press, 2002.

Von Speyr, Adrienne. *They Followed His Call: Vocation and Asceticism.* New York: Alba House, 1995.

Wald, Kenneth D., Dennis E. Owen, and Samuel S. Hill. "Churches as Political Communities." *American Political Science Review* 82 (1988): 531–48.

———. "Political Cohesion in Churches." *Journal of Politics* 52 (1990): 197–215.

Welch, Susan. "Women as Political Animals? A Test of Some Explanations for Male-Female Political Participation Differences." *American Journal of Political Science* 21 (1977): 711–30.

Wellman, James K. *The Gold Coast Church and the Ghetto: Christ and Culture in Mainline Protestantism.* Urbana: University of Illinois Press, 1999.

Willard, Frances E. *Woman in the Pulpit.* Chicago: Woman's Christian Temperance Publication Association, 1889.

Williams, Rhys H., ed. *Cultural Wars in American Politics: Critical Reviews of a Popular Myth.* New York: Aldine de Gruyter, 1997.

Wood, James R. *Leadership in Voluntary Organizations: The Controversy over Social Action in Protestant Churches.* New Brunswick: Rutgers University Press, 1981.

Wuthnow, Robert. *Acts of Compassion: Caring for Others and Helping Ourselves.* Princeton: Princeton University Press, 1991.

———. "Beyond Quiet Influence? Possibilities for the Protestant Mainline." In Robert Wuthnow and John H. Evans, eds., *The Quiet Hand of God: Faith-Based Activism and the Public Role of Mainline Protestantism.* Berkeley: University of California Press, 2002.

———. "The Moral Minority." *The American Prospect* 11 (22 May 2000).

———. *The Restructuring of American Religion: Society and Faith since World War II.* Princeton: Princeton University Press, 1988.

Zikmund, Barbara Brown. "Women and Ordination." In Rosemary Skinner Keller and Rosemary Radford Ruether, eds., *In Our Own Voices: Four Centuries of American Women's Religious Writing.* Louisville: Westminster John Knox, 1995.

Zikmund, Barbara Brown, Adair T. Lummis, and Patricia Mei Yin Chang. *Clergy Women: An Uphill Calling.* Louisville: Westminster John Knox, 1998.

Zuckerman, Phil. *Strife in the Sanctuary: Religious Schism in a Jewish Community.* Walnut Creek, CA: Alta Mira Press, 1999.

Index

abortion, 70, 79, 82, 87, 88, 104, 120–121, 142
action agendas, 24–25, 77–99. *See also* organizational mobilization or pressure; political context, influence on action agendas; political principles, influence on action agendas
advocacy strategies, 101, 103, 104, 110, 112–118, 122–123, 124, 127, 131–132
African American, 4, 47, 63
African Methodist Episcopal Church (AME), 5
agenda. *See* action agendas; issue agenda; political priorities; public agenda
AIDS. *See* HIV/AIDS
Alinsky, Saul, 116
American Baptist, 16, 39, 43, 45–46, 48, 50, 52–53, 63, 66, 70, 73, 87, 94, 103, 115
American Baptist Church's Office of Government Relations, 115
Antiwar activism, 15
approval of political activities, 103–108, 109–114, 115–116, 118–119, 120–121, 122, 144–145. *See also* church-state separation; political principles
Assemblies of God, 18

Baptist Joint Committee on Public Affairs, 48
Blumer, Herbert, 75–78
boycott, 110, 115, 131, 144

Brown, Antionette, 4
Brown, Olympia, 4

calling, 12, 28, 35–42, 55, 129, 145; to discuss politics, 28, 36–37, 55; to educate, 38–39, 42; to take political action, 28, 40–41
campaigning. *See* church-state separation; cue-giving, partisan cues; electoral strategies; endorsing candidates
Carroll, Jackson, 58
Catholic. *See* Roman Catholic
Charitable Choice, 10, 31, 118, 120, 124, 146
Chaves, Mark, 5, 52
Christian Church (Disciples of Christ), 4, 16, 29, 40, 43, 45–46, 50, 53, 63, 70, 92–93, 94, 95, 97, 98, 144
Christian Methodist Episcopal Church (CME), 5
Church and the Second Sex, The, 5
Church of the Nazarene, 18
church-state separation, 64, 103, 108–109, 119, 121, 140
civil rights movement, 11
clergy-laity gap, 13, 29, 128–129, 130–131, 132–133, 141, 146
clergy peer influence, 126–127, 128, 129, 132
Clinton, President Bill, 67–68
community organizing, 79, 81, 82, 110, 115–116, 131
congregational influence, 13, 19, 20, 29–30, 40, 41, 52, 53, 65, 66, 89, 91–95, 99,

104–105, 107, 108, 113, 114, 116, 126,
127, 128, 129, 130–131, 132–133, 140, 141,
142, 147
Conservative Judaism, 5, 12, 16, 18, 43,
63–64, 145–146
contacting public officials, 110, 115, 131
context. *See* local politics; political context
Cooperative Clergy Project, 17, 18, 19, 21,
50, 60, 80, 82, 106, 110–111, 125–127
Creech, Rev. Jimmy, 61, 72, 114
crime. *See* violence/crime
cue-giving, 24, 37, 100, 102; advocacy
cues, 103–104; electoral cues, 103;
multivariate analysis of, 125, 126–130;
partisan cues, 103–104, 112–113. *See also*
endorsing candidates; sermons on political issues; study groups
culture wars, 3

Daly, Mary, 5
denominations. See mainline Protestantism; religious traditions; *specific denomination name (e.g., American
Baptist)*
direct-action, 100, 141; multivariate analysis of, 125, 127, 130–132. *See also* advocacy strategies; electoral strategies;
partnership strategies
discrimination, 55, 59–60, 63, 65, 71–72,
74, 75, 78, 84–89, 90, 91, 92–93, 95,
97–98, 137, 138, 139, 141, 146. *See
also* gay rights; gender, and professional status; homosexuality; racism;
women's equality/rights
Djupe, Paul, 11
domestic violence. *See* violence/crime
Durkheim, Emile, 33, 34, 42, 55

economic development, 80, 81, 82, 93, 98,
111, 119, 142
economic justice. *See* hunger; poverty;
social justice
education: as political issue, 59–60, 79,
80, 81, 82, 117, 119. *See also* calling, to
educate; socialization, in seminary
electoral strategies, 24, 101, 103, 108–112,

127, 130–132. *See also* cue-giving, partisan cues; endorsing candidates
endorsing candidates, 105–106, 110. *See
also* cue-giving, partisan cues; electoral strategies
Episcopal Church and ministers, 5, 16,
39, 43, 46–47, 70, 73, 95, 97, 103, 109, 117
Episcopal Church's Office of Government Relations, 48
Evangelical Lutheran Church in America
and ministers, 16, 40, 43, 46, 47, 50, 53,
70, 71, 87, 104, 114, 117
evangelical Protestantism, 143; and ordination of women, 5–6, 18

faith-based initiatives, 15, 31, 101, 120, 124.
See also Charitable Choice; government partnerships; partnership strategies
family: as political issue, 59–60, 64, 66,
70. *See also* work/family balance
feminism or feminist ideology, 5, 6, 27,
30, 57–58, 62–63, 75, 139, 146, 147
feminization of the clergy, 7, 56, 145–147
food pantries. *See* hunger

Gamaliel Foundation, 116
gay rights, 38, 59–61, 72, 79, 82, 87–88, 122
gender, 12, 20, 21, 22, 25–26, 30; and leadership style, 41, 53, 55; and professional
status, 4, 7–8, 12–13, 30, 31, 38, 48, 51,
52, 53–54, 63, 73, 90, 91, 95–96, 122–
123, 138, 146; and workplace dynamics,
9–10, 20–21, 28; as asset, 3, 53–55, 56,
97–98, 137; as constraint, 3, 21, 30, 49–
53, 56, 123, 137; as disadvantage to upward mobility, 3, 50, 52; influence on
action agenda, 94; influence on political priorities, 23, 68–76; influence on
political strategies, 122–123, 134. *See
also* male clergy comparisons; socialization; work/family balance
gender gap, 3, 9
Gilbert, Christopher, 11
Goldsmith, Stephen, 124
government partnerships, 24, 31. *See also*

Charitable Choice; faith-based initiatives; implementation; partnership strategies
Greater Indianapolis Church Federation, 117
Guth, James, 11, 23, 43, 57, 89, 100

Hansen, John Mark, 28, 77, 87
health/healthcare: as a political issue, 59–60; 70. See also abortion
Hebrew Union, 48
hierarchical structure: influence on political choices of clergy, 53
HIV/AIDS, 59, 80, 88, 123
homelessness. See poverty
homosexuality, 37–38, 48, 68, 71, 80, 84, 88, 92–93, 114. See also gay rights
hunger, 37, 46–47, 59–60, 79, 80, 82, 87, 111, 115, 116, 121. See also poverty
Hunter, James Davison, 3, 145

ideology, 27; liberal, 3, 19–20, 22, 27, 57–58, 65, 73, 75, 145, 146–147
implementation, 15, 117, 118, 120. See also local politics; partnership strategies
Indianapolis, 16, 18, 117, 123–124
Industrial Areas Foundation, 116, 142. See also community organizing; Omaha Together One Community; Washington Interfaith Network
issue agenda, 25. See also action agendas; political priorities; public agenda
issue mobilization, 24, 78, 87, 88, 91. See also priority-action agenda comparison

Jelen, Ted, 11, 39
Judaism and rabbis, 18, 20–21, 34–35, 43, 48, 50, 53, 54, 63, 70, 90, 91, 93, 96, 97, 103, 109, 113, 115, 119, 122, 139, 140. See also Conservative Judaism; Reform Judaism

Kanter, Rosebeth Moss, 10
Kingdon, John, 66

letter to editor, 110, 113–114, 131
Lewinsky, Monica, 67–68
liberal. See ideology, liberal; liberal theology
liberal theology, 23, 145–146
local politics, 31–32, 40–41, 97–98, 112, 115–116, 118, 119, 138, 142. See also community organizing; economic development; Indianapolis; Milwaukee; Omaha; political context; Washington, D.C.
Lutheran. See Evangelical Lutheran Church in America and ministers

mainline Protestantism, 3, 12, 18, 20–21, 34–35, 39–40, 63, 64, 83–84, 93, 96, 122, 139, 140, 143, 145–146. See also American Baptist; Christian Church (Disciples of Christ); Episcopal Church and ministers; Presbyterian Church (U.S.A.); religious traditions; socialization; social justice; United Methodist Church and ministers
male clergy comparisons, 107, 109–110, 119, 121, 141, 145
Methodist. See United Methodist Church and ministers
Milwaukee, 16, 18, 46, 117, 124
Milwaukee Innercity Congregations Allied for Hope (MICAH), 116
minority. See African American; discrimination; gender, and professional status; racism
Mott, Lucretia, 4

Nebraskans Against the Death Penalty, 116
Nie, Norman, 57
Niebuhr, H. Richard, 43
norms. See gender; political principles; socialization, and the profession

Olson, Laura, 11
Omaha, 16, 18, 47, 61, 72, 114, 123, 124
Omaha Together One Community (OTOC), 116
organizational demobilization, 24, 29,

107, 113–114, 131, 132–133, 140, 141. *See
also* clergy-laity gap; congregational
influence; gender, professional status;
organizational mobilization or pressure
organizational mobilization or pressure,
24, 25, 28–31, 43–44, 45, 78, 84, 86, 98–
99, 138, 140, 141, 143, 145; on action
agendas, 29, 102; on political priorities, 64–66; on political strategy, 29,
112, 116, 132–133; on priority-action
agenda comparison, 91–96, 98–99.
See also congregational influence; organizational demobilization; religious
traditions

parachurch organizations, 142
partnership strategies, 101, 111, 118–120,
124, 127, 131–132. *See also* Charitable
Choice; faith-based initiatives; government partnerships
party affiliation, 19, 23
Pentecostal churches/Pentecostalism, 6,
18, 143
People of Indianapolis Seeking Economic Development (POISED), 116
political activities, 14–16, 40, 137, 138, 143.
See also action agendas; advocacy
strategies; approval of political activities; boycott; community organizing;
contacting public officials; cue-giving;
direct-action; economic development;
electoral strategies; implementation;
letter to editor; local politics; partnership strategies; sermons on political
issues
political context, 18–19, 20, 25, 30, 142,
143; influence on action agendas, 96–
99; influence on political priorities,
66–68; influence on political strategies, 102, 108, 112, 123–124, 128–129;
influence on priority-action comparison, 96–98, 99. *See also* Indianapolis;
local politics; Milwaukee; Omaha;
Washington, D.C.
political issues, 16, 32. *See also* abortion;
action agendas; discrimination; edu-

cation; family; gay rights; health/
healthcare; HIV/AIDS; hunger; issue agenda; political priorities; poverty; public agenda; racism; women's
equality/rights
political mobilization, 11, 13, 16, 20–21,
22–23, 25, 32, 125–132. *See also* clergy
peer influence; congregational influence; issue mobilization; organizational demobilization; organizational
mobilization or pressure; religious
traditions; religious traditions, organizations within; social justice,
mission
political principles, 25, 26–28, 32, 78, 91,
98–99, 138, 143, 144–145; influence on
action agendas, 83, 102; influence on
political priorities, 62–64; influence
on political strategies, 27–28, 108,
112–115, 126, 127; influence on priority-
action agenda comparison, 89–91,
98–99. *See also* approval of political
activities; social justice, mission
political priorities, 23, 24–25, 32, 42, 57–
76. *See also* gender, influence on political priorities; organizational mobilization pressure, on political priorities;
political context, influence on political priorities; political issues; political
principles, influence on political priorities; priority-action agenda comparison; public agenda, influence on
political priorities
political socialization. *See* socialization
political strategies, 16, 22, 24–25, 32, 100–
133. *See also* advocacy strategies; approval of political activities; boycott;
community organizing; contacting
public officials; cue-giving; direct-
action; economic development;
electoral strategies; implementation;
letter to editor; local politics; partnership strategies; sermons on political
issues
politics, 25, 31–32. *See also* local politics;
political context

poverty: as a political issue, 46–47, 55, 59–
60, 65–66, 70–71, 74, 79, 80, 81, 82, 83–
89, 90, 91, 95, 105, 107, 111, 116, 120, 121,
122, 124, 146
Preisand, Sally, 5
Presbyterian Church (U.S.A.) and ministers, 16, 38–39, 43, 51, 65, 70, 71, 73, 87,
88, 90, 92, 95, 97–98, 144
priority-action agenda comparison, 22,
23–24, 81–99; consistency, 83–88; inconsistency, 85, 88–89. *See also* organizational mobilization or pressure,
on priority-action agenda comparison; political context, influence on
priority-action comparison; political principles, influence on priority-
action agenda comparison; recruitment, influence on priority-action
comparison
pro-choice activism. *See* abortion
public agenda, 25, 66–68, 74, 75–76, 142;
influence on political priorities, 66–68
public stands on issues. *See* advocacy
strategies; cue-giving; sermons on
political issues

qualitative analysis; discussion of benefits, 22, 143–144

racial injustice. *See* racism
racism, 37, 55, 59–61, 71, 79, 80, 82, 84, 87–
88, 98, 116–117. *See also* discrimination
recruitment, 24, 26, 31, 78, 96–99, 142,
144, 145; influence on political strategies, 124; influence on priority-action
comparison, 96–98, 99. *See also* Indianapolis; local politics; Milwaukee;
Omaha; political context; Washington, D.C.
Reform Judaism, 5, 12, 16, 18, 43, 145–146
Religious Action Center of Reform Judaism, 48
religious institutions. *See* congregational
influence; religious traditions, organizations within; socialization, in seminary

religious organizational pressures. *See*
congregational influence; organizational demobilization; organizational
mobilization or pressure; religious traditions; religious traditions, organizations within; socialization, within religious traditions and the profession;
socialization in seminary
religious right, 64, 119. *See also* evangelical Protestantism
religious traditions, 33–35, 42, 43–48, 91,
147; organizations within, 29, 30, 41,
42–56, 92, 116–117, 122, 131, 133, 137,
140; women's caucus, 29. *See also*
congregational influence; Judaism
and rabbis; mainline Protestantism;
socialization, within religious traditions and the profession; socialization, in seminary; *specific names of
denominations (e.g., American Baptist)*
reproductive choice. *See* abortion
Roman Catholic, 2, 5–6, 18, 143
Rosenstone, Steven, 28, 77, 87

Sapiro, Virginia, 9
Sargeant, Kimon Howland, 3, 145
Schlozman, Kay Lehman, 9
Seneca Falls Convention, 2,4
sermons on political issues, 105–108, 126,
128, 130
Smidt, Corwin, 17
socialization, 9, 27, 69; in seminary, 12, 27,
43, 45, 64, 65, 69, 74, 90; on the job,
27, 45, 69; within religious traditions
and the profession, 11, 43, 45, 55, 74,
89–90. *See also* congregational influence; political principles; social justice, mission; social justice, tradition
social justice, 32, 34, 37, 40, 43, 45, 77–78,
117, 123, 126, 127; mission, 16, 21, 26–27,
33, 35, 56, 61, 74–75, 86, 108, 113, 128,
129, 137, 138; tradition, 12, 23, 64, 65,
72, 74, 79, 103–104, 112–113. *See also*
discrimination; gay rights; hunger;
poverty; racism
Society of Friends (Quakers), 4

stained glass ceiling, 75. *See also* gender, as disadvantage to upward mobility
study groups, 105–107, 126, 129, 130
suffrage. *See* women's equality/rights, to vote

temperance movement, 5
theology. *See* Judaism, and rabbis; mainline Protestantism; political principles; social justice, tradition
time pressures, 8, 30, 41, 86–87, 89, 93–94, 95, 107, 119, 129, 133, 141, 142

Union of American Hebrew Congregations, 48
Unitarian Universalists, 4
United Methodist Church and ministers, 5, 16, 43, 47, 50, 65, 68, 70, 71–72, 88, 92, 93–94, 95, 104–105, 109, 113; Document on Social Principles, 43
United (northern) Presbyterians, 5
United Presbyterian Church in the United States, 5

values. *See* political principles; socialization; social justice
Verba, Sidney, 57
violence/crime, 59–60, 67, 79, 80, 82, 111, 117–118, 121, 138
vocation. *See* calling

Washington, D.C., 16, 18, 53, 54, 124; lobbying offices in, 43, 47–48
Washington Interfaith Network (WIN), 116
Willard, Frances, 2
Women in the Pulpit, 2
Women's Christian Temperence Union, 2
women's equality/rights, 2, 5, 37, 64, 82, 84, 87–88, 116, 122; to vote, 4–5. *See also* discrimination; women's ordination
women's ordination, 2–3, 5–7, 90; arguments against, 2; arguments for, 2
work/family balance, 51, 93, 96–97. *See also* time pressures

Zikmund, Barbara Brown, 27